The

POWER

of the

VALLEY

Dr. Jacqueline Evans-Phillips

DEDICATION

This book is dedicated to a celebration of the legacy of my "Granny," Mary Theodora Ethelda Lebrun, December 5, 1925- July 24, 2018. Her legacy is one of significant depth and breadth.

She was a very simple yet powerful woman who moved mountains for her family. From toiling the soil in St. Lucia to paving pathways for us to immigrate and settle in the United States, Granny made tremendous sacrifices for her family up to the very end, all in the name of love.

We thank God for you, for your life, and for choosing you to be the matriarch of our lineage. We thank you for all your love and the sacrifices you made for each and every one of us in your simple way. You have instilled in us values and virtues that will go very deep and wide, and will carry your simple message of love through many generations. We will continue to honor your legacy by practicing the virtues in 1 Corinthians 13:4-8.

I love you, Granny.

TABLE OF CONTENTS

MY SEASON OF TRANSFORMATION 1

Dr. Jackie E. Phillips

THROUGH THE VALLEY 5

Sonya Weir

CHAPTER 2 7

What is The Valley?

Dr. Jackie E. Phillips

HIS POEM 17

Kennisha Flewellen

CHAPTER 3 21

Catch A Falling Star

Ainsworth Thompson

MEN ROSE 27

Sonya Weir

CHAPTER 4 29

Look Up

T'challa Williams

CHAPTER 5 37

Finding Ms. Lady

Jarmaine V. Lee

BREAKTHROUGH 45

Sonya Weir

CHAPTER 6 47

Set Back To Be Set Up

Madonna Lilburn-Thompson

Ruby There is purpose in your problem & pain.
Madonna Lilburn Thompson

CHAPTER 7 57

Forgiveness

Monique Taylor

GREATNESS WITHIN 61

Sonya Weir

CHAPTER 8 65

The Fight

K. Stephen Wilson

CHAPTER 9 73

Narcissistic Love

Sascia Hayden

MY SEASON OF TRANSFORMATION
Dr. Jackie E. Phillips

When God is ready to take you to a higher calling in your life, he creates a radical shift, which switches life as usual into a crisis. July 2014 was such a period in my life when my world came tumbling down. On the heels of divorce after 17 years of marriage, I became unemployed. Totally stripped from the security of a marriage and a full-time job, I received the directive to start my own business, Life Changers Consulting, LLC. This was a season of total surrender, obedience, and a faith walk; a season where I put my faith into action, confirming the statement that *the Lord will take care of all my needs*. A year and a half later, I can testify that I am a testimony to that statement, because he definitely did.

I had a three-year grace period to start my company before I totally lost my employment. Within that period, I bargained with God, worrying that my business would not be able to sustain me and I needed to find another full-time job. I became persistent in that direction while at the same time, moved forward in growing the business. June 30, 2017, my last day of full-time employment, came around. None of my efforts towards getting a full-time job had materialized. It was, indeed, a time of mixed and ambivalent feelings. It was fear of the unknown; but trust in my God "got my back." The words of God kept ringing in my spirit, "Do you trust me?" This was a season of reliving the words of the 23rd Psalm, "The Lord is My Shepherd," and how God provided for me during that troublesome season of my life. The first six months after losing my job were the most challenging, comprising both high and low experiences, some of which occurred simultaneously. Financially, I was struggling, getting behind on my bills, and increasing my debt. However, I also got many opportunities to expand my business and **Soar into Greatness**.

Being sandwiched between both experiences didn't allow me to stay in the valley for too long. I was able to see my breakthrough and capitalized on the resources and support from my **Village**. A sense of joy stabilized me and prevented me from sinking deep down into the valley. In addition, I was able to invest in two wonderful coaches who have guided me toward growing and developing my business. Today, I am on the other side of that crisis. Yes, I may feel that I may not be where I want to be financially. But God reminds me to continue trusting him and I am confident he always feeds his sheep.

To accomplish his will, God will strip you, and begin transformative work within you. The stripping process signals the hallmark of a crisis in your life. The pain and turmoil associated with our valley experiences can sometimes create a depressive state in people. Without the right support and resources, many people may remain stuck in their valley experiences for several years. Getting to the other side of the journey is indeed a transformation and one through which I can usher individuals.

My mission as a **Mid-Wife of Purpose** is to empower people to live a life of purpose by **Soaring into Greatness**. In doing so, I awaken individuals to the healing and transformative sides of their life story. In my **Soaring into Greatness Institute©**, I use writing as a tool, where my clients write, share, and publish their life stories to create a sense of healing within themselves, then bless the lives of others. Through this nine-month process, they deconstruct their journey to define meaning and purpose to each participant's narrative. The outcome of this process is a book project compilation of their stories. This book you now hold, **The Power of the Valley,** is the second of The Dr. Jackie's Book Project. I am currently recruiting for my third endeavor as I compile this book.

In **The Power of the Valley**, you will get to read fifteen accounts from my contributing authors who all completed the **Soaring into**

Greatness Institute©. Their stories illustrate the power they found in their valleys, describing their resiliency and transformation. Taking this bold step by writing and sharing their stories was not an easy process. But with determination they persisted. They all revisited their trauma and their pain, pushing past the shame and guilt that may have been associated with their stories. Their nine-month journey was marked by the following steps as they processed and wrote their depictions of how they each came to understand the meaning of the **Power** of their valleys:

1. Identify the point of impact and events that led up to the crisis.
2. Evaluate their state of mind while they experienced emotional paralysis.
3. Recognize when they reached a breakthrough of hope during their valley experience.
4. List what strategies and support they used to diminish the symptoms of the crisis.
5. Analyze where they are on the journey towards **Wholeness**. Have they moved into a stage of healing, restoration, and renewal?
6. What are the energy blocks or dead areas that are showing up in their lives?
7. Discover what a **Season of Harvest** means to their story? How can they enhance or develop a platform to create impact and share their story and talents in the marketplace?

My mission is not only for my authors, but to empower as many people as possible. There is power and healing in our valley experiences. Going through a valley event is not an easy journey. Such an occurrence requires persistence, determination, faith, endurance, and support. In pushing through, we can get to the other side as renewed and transformed persons. Such a transformation brings a restored mindset that reveals the need to lean toward a life of greatness and service. Further, surviving a major life crisis prepares you for other crises which will indeed show up in your life. The blessing you receive is that your resiliency and rate of recovery will be much faster in moving through your valley.

My journey has become my story, one of transformation, healing, and wholeness. Being obedient to God's will and trusting in the process will help bring us to the **Other Side**. How has your journey transformed your life's story? The account is yours to tell and will bless the lives of others. Have you found meaning from your valley experiences? Or are you having difficulty navigating through your valley? To help your process and answer these questions, my mission is to provide a **Roadmap** for you to understand the concept of the valley and the stages of transformation that occur during this process.

Therefore, as you journey through this book, I would like you to:

a) Understand the **Power of the Valley** model and identify your personal stage of transformation.

b) Enjoy and read the 15 stories and poems in this book. From the stories, identify strategies that you can use immediately in your own life.

c) Develop plans and actions to help you push through your current phase and move onto the next.

d) Connect with me if you have any questions or would like to be part of the **Soaring into Greatness Institute** at **info@drjackiephillips.com**

Blessings,

Dr. Jackie

THROUGH THE VALLEY

Sonya Weir

Yea, though I walk
Through the valley of broken pieces,
Sweltering furnace, plagues and
diseases, Bruised, scratched and burnt,
Still, I didn't get down.

Yea, though I slink
Through the valley of
Depression and oppression,
And oft' times stumble in my imperfection,
I look to God for new direction.

Yea, though I walk
Through the valley of
Hurts and pain,
I pray to God
To find new life again.

Yea, though I tread
Through the valley
Of mistrust and disbelief,
Unbarred, I look to God and In
Him I find relief.

Yea, though I walk
Through the valley of
Sin and shame, beggary and adultery, insanity and
vanity, Drudgery and catastrophe, miseducation,
abortions and fornication, being misunderstood, rotten

neighborhoods, rejection, addiction, conflictions… I
stayed unhooked.

Yea, though I stand
In the valley and look
At my past and all that "could,"
The shame, near fame
And unfair games,
I'm thanking God he kept me sane.

Yea, though I walk
Through the valley of lack,
I'm thanking God and I won't look back.
Yea, though I walk
From the valley renewed
With gratitude and new attitude.

Yea, though I walked
From the valley of bones,
God is with me;
I am never alone.
In the valley,
He restoreth My soul.

CHAPTER 2

What is The Valley?

Dr. Jackie E. Phillips

Last year, my first book project, **Soaring into Greatness** illustrated the stories of my contributing authors, fifteen who pushed through adversities to soar to the mountaintops of their lives. In preparing for Book Project II, I felt completed to trace the journey of the **Seed of Greatness** that propels us to **Soar**. To understand that our life journey is made up of highs and lows and for the context of this book, mountains and valleys, I was guided by the Spirit to focus on the valley, a low land between two mountaintops. According to Webster's Dictionary, a valley is a low area between hills or mountains, often with a river running through it. This geological formation can either be U- or V-shape, generally longer than wider.

Why is it that some people can soar up to the mountain tops while others remain stagnant in the valley? The answer to that question was very beneficial to me as a **Mid-Wife of Purpose**, as I seek to empower others to transition through the valley and **Soar into Greatness**. My nine-month journey began, on assignment from the Spirit, and was coupled with much research and collaboration with my contributing authors at the **Soaring into Greatness Institute**. The outcome of this process is the compilation of this book. The added practical value to you is the development of **The Power of the Valley Model©**.

The Power of the Valley Model©

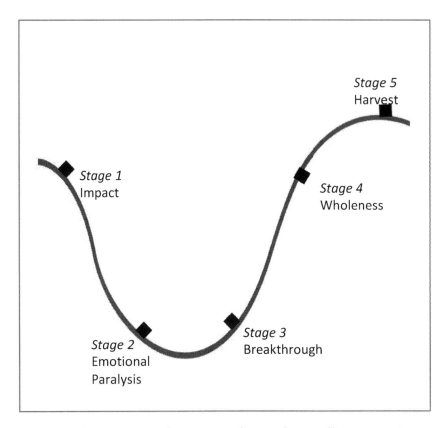

Fig. 1: The stages of moving through a valley experience

The Power of the Valley Model© illustrates the five stages of transformation you pass through from moment of impact by a crisis to the ascent of soaring to your next mountain top. Each stage happens both in your conscious and your subconscious. The conscious level illustrates the actions you take as you endure the turmoil associated with the crisis.

The subconscious transformation demonstrates the development of a **Seed of Greatness** which carries the tools needed for your next mountain top assignment. The development of **The Seed of Greatness** is measured by your mindset and actions taken in the conscious level. The subconscious transformation gives birth to the Seed of Greatness that will enable you to soar to your next mountain top. Therefore, it is very important for that seed to develop and grow and germinate. In this framework, I will be using the context of germination of the seed into a tree to illustrate how the **Seed of Greatness** enables you to soar to your next mountain top. I use the analogy of germination to show how that seed will mature, progress into a sprout, and develop into a tree that will bear fruit in your final stage out of your valley experience. Processing this transformation and making meaning of your journey during crisis can be very difficult for some. Therefore, as I highlight each stage below, I will illustrate the conscious and subconscious transformations that will occur.

The length and time in each phase will vary from person to person. Progressing through each stage takes place on a continuum with the goal of moving through the five stages. How you move through each stage determines your actions of being stagnant, sporadic, or consistent and intentional. These actions are measured on a **Progression Scale** from **0 - 5** with level **0** being no activity and level **5** demonstrating intentional and consistent actions within that stage. Being stagnant for lengthy periods indicates the need for external support and resources. You may have maxed out the use of your own abilities to push through the situation. **The Power of the Valley Model©** provides the support and resources you need.

Progression Scale: 0-5

- Performing at a Level 0 indicates no action or stagnation.

- Level 3 shows that you are taking action, but only sporadically.

- Level 5 demonstrates intentional, consistent actions.

Stage 1 - Impact

At the conscious level:

This is the moment of impact when you collide with a life defining situation. The impact creates a crisis, pushes you down and begins the descent into **The Valley**. You will ask such questions as, "Why Me? What did I do to deserve this? This is totally unfair." Such emotions can skew your perception and can alter how you process the situation. Therefore, your mindset plays a critical role, as it determines how you view the impact. If you see the impact as a hopeless situation, then the recovery rate will be much longer because it seems like your world is experiencing total disaster. This first stage sets the tone for the next transition.

You may have prior warning of the moment of impact in some situations. When you see an impending problem, you are at an advantage because the duration at **Stage 2** will be shorter than those without prior awareness. Impact begins the rapid descent into Stage Two. What is measured at this stage is your state of mind and how you will react to the crisis.

At the subconscious level:

There is a **Seed of Greatness** associated with the crisis illustrated in the conscious level of this stage. When the impact occurs, the seed is released in you. Implantation of that seed will occur, based on the nature of the soil (your mind set), your environment, and the elements needed for germination of this seed of greatness. All of those elements are impacted based on your actions at the conscious level.

Stage 2 - Emotional Paralysis

At the conscious level:

During this time, you feel helpless, tired, and lack motivation. Your emotions keep you trapped in crisis; you feel a sense of hopelessness due to the severe impact. This is the lowest and darkest point of **The Valley**. Your journey during this phase may last from an hour to many years. As you journey through this stage, an increase level of actions will push you through this stage. You will move from a state of no action to a level 5 of activity. The increased activity will then transition you into the next stage of **Breakthrough**. The mindset begins to transform, moving from a stage of paralysis to random, then intentional, and finally consistent action, which marks the beginning of the next phase.

On the other hand, if your actions are at a level two for an extensive number of months, an external intervention needs to occur. You will need to seek additional support. If no support is provided, you may enter a stage of depression.

At the subconscious level:

During the second stage in **The Valley**, the implantation of the seed is contingent on your mindset at the impact stage. Your low energy level experienced during this stage will force the seed to become dormant until you begin to take action at the conscious level by improving your mindset and understanding the elements of the crisis. If your actions remain at a level two or under for an extensive period, and no external support is provided, your **Seed of Greatness** will die and be miscarried. When the seed is aborted, you will continue to exist in **The Valley**. Eventually, you will encounter a new crisis and the downward cycle will continue. It may take you several attempts of going through the first two phases of this cycle until a breakthrough can occur.

Conversely, someone who progresses from a level three toward a level five will foster the seed to progress in its germination stage toward becoming a full-grown plant. The goal of your **Seed of Greatness** is to develop into a tree that will bear fruit and give you the tools needed for your next mountain top assignment. The next stage for your **Seed of Greatness** as it germinates will be the **Breakthrough** stage.

Stage 3 - The Breakthrough

At the conscious level:

One of the main features of this stage is developing the necessary actions to climb out of **The Valley**. You will move on a continuum through this stage with consistent actions to seek support and identify a solution to your crisis. The journey in this stage may vary from a few months for some, to a lifetime for others. Progression through this phase marks the beginning of the end of the crisis, depending on the nature of the crisis, your renewed mindset, resources, and supporting structures. Actions you take during this phase will help mitigate the pain of the crisis. Based on these elements, fluctuation with moments of sporadic activity of consistent actions to moments of being stagnant is quite normal.

- As time passes, you may increase your action or remain stagnant with limited activity at level 2 or below. Becoming stagnant at this stage is also very possible, even if you are nearing the end of the crisis. With lack of solid support and resources, your activity will be limited to that level and may not be enough to put an end to your crisis. If no additional assistance is provided at this stage and after several months, a person may become depressed. Persistence and determination are the key elements to get

12

you through. In addition, continue to seek resources to guide you through these transitions.

- If you move towards the stage of mastery at a level four or five your actions, resources and support move you towards ending the crisis. In addition to ending your crisis, you will also notice a renewed mentality along with the desire to continue your positive actions. With such awareness you may decide to push onward to begin the passage toward **Wholeness** at Stage 4.

- Others may decide that achieving mastery is a goal they are satisfied with, especially if the crisis has come to an end. This level marks the exit from **The Valley** and the return to the status quo prior to the crisis. Despite an end to the symptoms of the crisis, emotional scars will still linger. These scars will serve as a reminder of the crisis that you have endured.

At the subconscious level:

Like all the other stages, the subconscious level stage mirrors the conscious level at this **Breakthrough** stage. Signs of transformation will become visible to you as you progress to mastery. Your **Seed of Greatness** is no longer a seed but has evolved into a plant on its journey to bear fruit in the next stages. As mentioned earlier, these fruits are the tools you will need for your next climb into a higher dimension.

- Individuals who have reached mastery at this level and are moving into the next stage of **Wholeness** will reach a deeper level of awareness of their transformation and will move towards **Soaring into Greatness** at a higher dimension.
- Individuals who have mastered this stage but decided to remain at that level will have attained some

13

transformation, but have decided to maintain the status quo. This level of success of a renewed mindset and ending the crisis is enough for many.

- Finally, for those who remain stagnant at this stage, a miscarriage of the **Seed of Greatness** will occur. Even if the seed has evolved towards being a plant, the elements are not enough to sustain its development towards the mastery of this stage.

Stage 4 - Wholeness

At the conscious level:

Stage 4 marks the beginning of the journey towards **Wholeness**. You will progress from a level one, to mastery at level five. The stage makes complete **The Valley** experience and the climb towards a higher mountaintop. During this phase, you will begin to understand that, even if the crisis no longer exists, emotional scars do linger. These scars remind you of the crisis you have endured. Upon completion of Phase 3, you may jump to **Wholeness** immediately or it might take years. Many people never get to this phase. By continuing to strive for it, you will experience a higher consciousness of forgiveness, release, renewal, and healing. You will understand that there can be a lesson learned with crisis. You will gain understanding about your growth into a stronger person because you survived the impact of crisis. It is in that realization that you now are on a mission to take the positive aspects of your journey and unhinge from the negativity. Like shedding skin, you can begin to forgive, and make strides toward releasing, renewal and healing. The transformation is powerful because at this point you can understand that there was a subconscious process going on at the same time as your determined actions on a conscious level.

At the subconscious level:

At this phase, the individual is fully conscious of the transformation that has transpired during the journey in The Valley. Their actions are now focused on fostering and strengthening that transformation. In moving through this stage, you will make intentional decisions of engaging in actions that will enhance the releasing of the negative aspects associated with trauma, and move forward with the fruits of the transformation. This period marks a major milestone wherein the subconscious and conscious levels merge. With this realization, you are now able to operate and engage in actions that will renew your spirit and the **Seed of Greatness** that is within you. With consistent progress, you will then move into the next stage of using fruits of greatness to create impact and live a life of purpose.

Stagnation in this stage may occur at levels 1 to 3 due to the intensity and turmoil of your crisis. Once you progress to levels 4 and 5, you are now in the realm of being truly whole.

Phase 5 – Harvest

Merging the conscious and the subconscious levels:

Mastering the stage of **Wholeness** brings you to the next stage of **Harvest**. There are two significant characteristics of this stage. **The Harvest** is the transformation of your seeds to fruits of **Greatness.** These fruits or tools are needed to make a difference in the lives of others. At this stage, you realize that your journey becomes your story. You will share this odyssey to empower others who are currently stuck in their valley experience. You are at a stage of using your story as a stool to develop a platform in the marketplace. Your actions in this stage are purposeful, intentional, and consistent in enhancing your spirit.

The second characteristic of this stage is that you are now on the summit of a higher mountaintop as compared to your past mountain. This new environment will produce its new challenges, valleys, and transitions. Your journey through your valley has prepared you for this new environment and the valley moments associated with these new adjustments. Your rate of recovery and time in **The Valley** become shorter as you are now conscious of the transformation each valley experience brings toward greatness. You will endure redefining yourself. Be intentional about creating a positive impact and making a difference in your life and the lives of others. Gain the wisdom that there is greatness within you and understand that you are meant to live a life of purpose.

HIS POEM

Kennisha Flewellen

I grew up in a life full of secrets
That follow me year by year;
Sometimes keeping them feels like regret,
But I never knew if I wanted anyone to hear.

People have come and gone in an instant,
Blowing away like the wind; So, I
wanted to keep myself distant,
Feeling like I was covered in sin.

Closed myself off from the world,
Never letting ones too close to me;
Trapped in a cage was that little girl,
Just wanting the key to set herself free.

I envied those that had that one. . .
That one they could always count on;
That one they thought was second to none,
Thought my chances of having that were gone.

I allowed some in to test the ride,
But they never seemed up to par.
I asked God to be my guide
And I let Him set my life's bar.

The things I did not want to believe He began to
reveal to me.
The things I did not want to conceive I actually
began to see.

But He had already seen my path

17

And aligned my steps accordingly;
Put things in motion that may have caused wrath,
But were things that had to be.

There was a friend he wanted me to know
One I didn't know, but didn't need to meet.
A friend I may have never known,
If he didn't remove me from that seat.

I never expected to find you
In the midst of the darkness and rain;
I never suspected you would also need me,
As we equally shared our pain.

To have an ear to listen, a shoulder to lean
When I didn't know where to turn;
Patience to spare when I wanted to be mean
Because my heart only felt the burn.

When I thought I wasn't worthy
He delivered you to me - no reason, no rhyme;
He had already seen what we couldn't see
#igotchu - my #root, my #lifetime.

"We are stronger in the places
we have been broken."
-Hemmingway

DR. JACKIE EVANS PHILLIPS

CHAPTER 3
Catch A Falling Star
Ainsworth Thompson

December 27th 2007 was finally here and I was on my way. Every year, I rewarded myself with a trip to Jamaica. My goal was to start and end the year on the island. There was nothing I looked forward to more than spending three weeks in paradise to celebrate a year of making money. My company was doing great, the money was pouring in, and I had a fat crib in the nicest part of the city. I was on top of the world and that was all that was important. As the plane landed, I peered out the window, soaking up the reality that I was back in paradise.

I was born in Jamaica and came to the U.S. when I was eight. Ever since then, I've always wanted to go back to live there. Since the economy is not great in Jamaica, the next best thing was to and visit there as much as possible. With my company doing so well, I could visit whenever I wanted . . . this was a real dream come true.

I woke up the following day, December 28th at my favorite place on the planet: a quaint, seductive villa in Negril called CATCH A FALLING STAR. I sat out on the front porch, allowing the cool island breeze to massage my skin while I gazed out on the sea before making my way down to breakfast.

The grounds at CATCH A FALLING STAR are stunning. Walking through the property is like walking through the Garden of Eden. Beautiful tile and stone paths lined with exotic plants and billowing blossoms creeped their way onto the path as you meander your way through the palace grounds. When I got to breakfast, my cousin and travel partner, Joe, was already there waiting for me.

The breakfast at CATCH A FALLING STAR is always official. We drank mimosas and enjoyed a delicious, authentic Jamaican breakfast while tycoon laughing about all the money we had made for the year.

After breakfast, we met up with my other cousin Mike, who lived on the island. We mapped out festivities for the coming days leading up to the New Year's Eve celebration. The party was on!

As usual, we spent New Year's Eve partying at WHITE SANDS BEACH CLUB. Live music, great cocktails, some seriously, seriously, seriously sexy women, and the party didn't stop until in the morning; you couldn't ask for more.

We partied all night, drinking champagne, and rum punch, and dancing to reggae music. We spent the first of the year relaxing on the beach, drinking and soaking up the island sun while meditating to the sounds of reggae music.

The next day, Wednesday, January 2, was the first business day of 2008. I called into my office to check in. My business manager, Jenny, told me something I never thought was possible. She explained that one of the banks we were using to fund our clients' loans had closed. I had never heard of a bank closing and never thought that was possible.

I was very surprised; we had 35 loans with this bank that needed to be funded. If these loans did not fund, this would change my business for the worse. I had to do something. I was thousands of miles away and my business was about to crumble. Immediately, I went into emergency mode. I grabbed my Rolodex to start calling my contacts at other banks. Everyone told me they would have to re-underwrite the loans to fund them, which would take much more time that we had to close them. After talking to just about every banker on my contact list, I made contact with John Shuster at AMERICAN FUNDING NETWORK. He assured me that he could use the existing paperwork to close the loans based on the approvals we already had. I put John in contact with my business manager to transfer the loans to AMERICAN FUNDING. Phew!! Emergency averted. John had saved the day. We were able to close on all the loans as planned, so I went back to my vacation.

When I returned to the United States and to work, I found out that three other banks had closed since I had left. This was weird, "Why were these banks closing?" I asked myself. I'd never heard of a bank closing. I have seen many banks get bought out by other banks, but had never seen any of them actually close. Within three months, eight more banks closed. Thankfully, AMERICAN FUNDING NETWORK was going strong and still closing loans for us. Business did slow down, but I did not really think anything of it other than maybe I needed to get out and do some more marketing.

I put on my marketing hat and got out there, shaking hands and networking. But business still did not pick up; in fact, it slowed down even more. I decided that I needed to ramp up the advertising to get more customers; but that didn't help either.

The real estate market was changing. It was slowing down and not as many people were interested in buying homes. Banks kept shutting down and the phone stopped ringing as frequently. Business was bad. And the few clients that I did get, I was not able to place their loans, because so many banks had closed. The ones that remained, tightened their lending guidelines so it was difficult to get clients who qualified for their loan. I had to start thinking about letting some of the staff go. It broke my heart when I had to tell the business manager, Jenny, that I had to let her go because business was so slow and I was no longer able to keep her on.

I eventually had to let everyone go, and by August, 2008, I closed the doors to my business for good. I was devastated and heartbroken, but I reasoned that the newspapers and magazines described this as just a natural part of the economic cycle and the market would turn around in time. Months passed by, nothing got better; it got much worse. The news reports said we were experiencing the worst recession since the Great Depression of the 1930's and it could get even worse. Large banks were now closing and eventually investment banks shut down.

The country was experiencing a financial collapse. None of the banks were lending money; there was a credit crunch and no one could access financing for anything. No one was doing business and everyone was afraid of what was happening with the economy.

I didn't have any money coming in, but the bills kept arriving. I had to turn to my investments to pay them. I liquidated some investment funds and used the money to pay expenses as I waited for the situation to get better. Only thing is, things didn't get better; they still kept spiraling down. Property foreclosures were coming in record numbers and people were filing bankruptcies to avoid losing their homes.

I survived until Christmas that year before I had to liquidate more investments to survive. No Jamaica trip this year; it was too expensive. In fact, I couldn't even afford to have my annual Christmas party. The situation was horrible. I had become quite depressed.

My family came for Christmas as they always did, but this year was different. The usual excitement was not there, the money was short, and festivities suffered.

It wasn't until everyone was ready to leave on December 27 when severe depression hit me. I had sunk to the lowest point I had ever been. I knew that everyone was about to leave and instead of boarding a plane to Jamaica, I would be all alone in my house, no office to go to, no friends visiting. I went to the third floor where I could be by myself. I sat in the window sill feeling as if my soul was being dragged down to the depths of Hell. A weighty feeling of foreboding came over me. I felt depressed, frightened, cold, and alone. I sat against the window and wept out loud, not knowing what would happen to me.

While I was up there crying, I heard my cousin call to me to say I should come down as the family was leaving. I dried my tears and made my way down to say goodbye to everyone.

After they left, I sat alone in silence until the next day. When I awoke, I felt like a completely different person. The idea that I didn't have a business and wasn't making any money didn't matter to me. The fact that I was all alone in a huge house didn't matter. That I wasn't going on my yearly vacation to Jamaica didn't bother me either. All I knew was that I needed to learn more about God.

I decided that I needed to go back to school at a seminary and get a degree in Divinity. I began researching enrollment into THE HARTFORD SEMINARY that was within walking distance from my home. I didn't know what I would do with a degree in Divinity or why I wanted to study. I felt like something was pushing me toward spirituality and this was the way to learn as much as I could about it. I knew that I wasn't interested in being a preacher, but learning about God was something I must do.

I enrolled at the seminary and began attending classes. I felt great about what I was doing. I didn't know where it would take me, but I felt liberated and in control of my life and destiny. I also felt like a totally different person than I had been before. I no longer valued money as all important. I began to see people differently, too. I had never considered what they thought or felt to be significant. I previously had considered empathy to be a waste of energy. Now, I began being concerned with the feelings of others and what was going on in their emotional lives.

I became a completely different person. It's as if Ainsworth 1.0 had died and Ainsworth 2.0 was born in the same instant. And the funny thing is, I don't miss 1.0 at all. In fact, I can now see what an arrogant, self-centered person he was. I am glad he is gone. My idea that materialism was the measure of a successful person completely changed. Now I want to help others and give back to society. It is unfortunate that I had to lose everything to come to this realization, but I am glad that it happened because I now see what the important things are in life and I feel much better about myself.

Now that I am back on my feet, I still try to go to Jamaica at least once a year; but if I can't make it there, it is no big deal. Life goes on. What has become important is being good to myself and doing good onto others. CATCH A FALLING STAR is still my favorite place on the planet, but now when I walk through the winding paths of flowers, I stop to smell them and truly appreciate their beauty and all of the amazing things God has blessed me with in this life. I have finally found perfect peace and my true paradise.

MEN ROSE

Sonya Weir

Facts!
Men rose, black men rose.
Black men making their comeback rose.
And I, witnessed as he rose and
Held my peacock gaze.
I stood amazed as
My son rose and walked;
He walked across the stage
At the announcement of his name
And I thought to myself
Another black man unchained,
Disrupting the status quo.
Glory to only God he owes,
And he smiled in nervous delight.
His professors praised,
Commenting that he was
Well raised, yes!
So are many
Young men his age.
My son, black sons, all sons,
Rose and walked
At the announcement of their names.
Parents' pride rose.
Another black man uncaged,
Disrupting the status quo,
Overcoming setbacks,
Making strong comeback
Promised futurity.
Facts! I supposed.

DR. JACKIE EVANS PHILLIPS

CHAPTER 4

Look Up

T'challa Williams

The valley is vast and beautiful, decorated with thick green grass beneath your feet, garnished by flowers of every color and sweet aromas floating on cool breezes all around you. Just as in life, there are seasons in the valley, cycles which exist to ensure we have learned and are wholly equipped to handle the challenges and experiences at the next level. Often, we only see people celebrating victories, which leaves us to assume how everything came to be. I'm going to give you a front seat to my development journey. There are certain moments in life that serve as a catalyst to pivotal seasons. 2011 was my year; a paradigm shift.

In that year, my church started a Bible school and the schedule was rigorous. Attending this school was something God called me to do. I knew the minute God places you in the direction of your purpose, the enemy comes to challenge your will and test your faith. We have a tendency to underestimate what this process entails. I thought since I was raised in the church and was now obtaining an in-depth knowledge of God's Word, I was ready for what the enemy had in store. In all honesty, we are never ready, because the enemy pursues our weaknesses; pride coupled with ego gives us a false sense of security. We get comfortable with our strengths and don't realize that development is a part of strengthening our weak areas. The valley then becomes a no-flex zone! But God is faithful; He will finish the work that He began in you.

January started off with the loss of my uncle. This was hard for everyone, especially my grandmother. She was burying her only son who she had loved deeply. Cancer was swift when it snuck up and aggressively snatched him. As my grandmother mourned, I worked hard to be her support and lead wherever I could. I know how to be there for other people and give sound advice, to other people. But when it comes to myself, advise is in short supply. I don't even consider my pain.

In June, my family had to move out of our apartment in one day in order to avoid going to court for rent. We managed to find a house in the same neighborhood. This was good, because no matter what we went through at home, I needed my children's school and friends to remain consistent. I preserved their circle. I wanted to make sure they could rely on that part of their life, no matter what we were facing as a family.

While we were in that house, we still had financial difficulties. I worked hard to make sure we still had family moments together in the midst of the madness. Laughter is such good medicine and it was the one thing my family continues to do together. My family consisted of my husband, our six children and me. Yeah, eight is enough! When I prayed, I would tell God that he had mad jokes as I looked at the size of my family. I was an only child and I had given birth to three boys and three girls. Who would have thought that? Please know, when I say struggle, I am not talking about a lightweight situation. I am talking about no utilities: lights off, gas off, water off, no food, and heart heavy all while looking at six children. Granted, all these things weren't happening at once but they were definitely tag teaming. On top of trying to maintain a home, my husband had congestive heart failure.

In August, my husband went to the hospital because he was retaining water. We were accustomed to that because it was part of his illness. Sometimes medication needed to be changed, but we would not know until his body told us. While he was sleeping, his irregular heartbeats caused so much concern that doctors immediately placed a defibrillator in his chest. That was scary! But soon he was home and recovering.

While he was recuperating, I received a phone call from my neighbor in Connecticut. She told me that my grandmother had fallen in the yard, was hurt, and was in the hospital. This broke my heart. Even though I was going through my own situation, this was the woman who had raised me and I was not able to be there for her. Our electricity was off and the rent was late. And I was tired. But I continued to work full time and go to Bible school on Tuesdays and Thursdays until 10:00pm and Saturday mornings from 8:00am to 12:00pm. I also served as a teacher for four- to six-year-olds on Sundays, all while taking the Metropolitan Atlanta Rapid Transit Authority. I rode from Decatur to Roswell to College Park. I was pouring into everyone I could because it gave me strength. I was very good at being strong for others, to avoid the pain I was going through. When God wants to take you to another level, you cannot continue to run from your pain. If you won't face it on your own, God will get you to a quiet place in the valley and he will develop you.

When I went to class, God was moving. I know He can move, I just had doubts that He was moving for me. Do you know that you can be so humble that it's almost pride? Let me explain. I was in class at Bible school and the subject was prosperity. In the midst of this, my power was off and my bill was more than a thousand dollars. The minister began to speak about how God is a provider and had told him he needed to bless some folks that night. He asked the class who needed help. This was my blessing, but shame is a powerful thing. I didn't want anyone to know. I felt my amount was too big to get help. I kept my mouth shut. Those who were brave enough to speak up had their bills paid on the spot. At the end of class, the minister said he had his check book ready because God had already spoken to him and told him this would be a great amount but the response he received wasn't what he was expecting. Someone was holding back. At that moment, I knew I had missed my blessing. That whole move of God was for me but I believed myself over God's word. Doubt had been louder than faith.

In October, I was giving a friend a ride to work. I saw the police officer parked in the cut and hoped he would not pursue me. But he did. Once he pulled me over, I gave him my information, yet still felt nervous. That's when the second car pulled up. I remember thinking, "Oh shit!" Yes, that was exactly what I thought as they removed me from the vehicle and proceeded to tell me that my license and registration was suspended for a failure to appear for a traffic violation. Damn. I had forgotten about that ticket from almost a year prior.

When I got to court, they would not let me out on my own recognizance because I had failed to appear previously. I was going to sit in DeKalb county until Monday. I was arrested at 8:00am on Friday. This was going to be a long weekend. Jail is an awful, nasty place to be. In booking, I was in the company of other older women on traffic violations; a pregnant teenager who was being held as an adult (that seemed so wrong to me); and a girl in a suit charged with murder. To put a cherry on the top, *First 48* was filming. Who in the hell wants to have their face float by on *First 48*? That didn't matter, my mugshot was already public record.

I hated putting their non-fitting underwear and orange uniform on my body. It was cold, very cold. My bed was a slab of metal because there were no more mattresses (which were more like elementary gym mats than Sealy Posturepedic)! I had a sheet for a blanket in a place that used cold as a type of punishment. I was praying and working hard to maintain my peace. But the pressure of the entire year was starting to weigh on me. I missed my husband and my babies and just wanted to be done with this whole ordeal. As I went to my cell, to my surprise there was a booklet from my church that my cellmate had on her desk! It had grapes on the cover and was talking about the Fruit of the Spirit. I got chills when I saw this because the lesson that we were studying in one of my classes was the Fruit of the Spirit and this week's topic was long-suffering. When I saw that booklet, I said, "Okay, God. You definitely have my attention. I am listening."

There is always something to learn in the valley to develop and strengthen you. The most important thing to remember is to be ready to learn. That is hard to do when you are being pressed on all sides. God's Word says, *"WE ARE TROUBLED ON EVERY SIDE BUT NOT DISTRESSED...FOR OUR LIGHT AFFLICTION, WHICH IS BUT FOR A MOMENT, WORKETH FOR US A FAR MORE EXCEEDING AND ETERNAL WEIGHT OF GLORY." II CORINTHIANS 4: 8-18*

My situation was temporary. I needed to keep God's word at the forefront of my mind and tell myself to hush. My fear and worry would create negative talk that would directly contradict God's promise. Our job as believers is to stand on the promises of God. He can't lie and he can't fail. I kept telling myself that all things work together for my good. (*ROMANS 8:28*).

I held onto my faith, avoided the drama and arguments that occurred all around me, and waited to be sent to the second county where my ticket was. Yes, I needed to go to TWO jails. If you can't be still, God will sit you still just to get you to your blessing! It was Wednesday and it was time for me to be moved. I was taken from my cell and given back my clothes as I waited with four other women for transport. I felt relieved because I was closer to being done with the whole ordeal. One by one, all the women in the cell were being picked up. I was the last one. I had gotten comfort from the idea of moving to the next jail and being able to go home. Being in the valley has nothing to do with the end, and everything to do with the journey through. I was in the midst of suffering long and not acknowledging my pain. I just wanted it to be done. God said, "No."

My transport did not come. I was told I needed to go get my orange suit back on and go back to jail. Do not pass Go. Do not collect two hundred dollars. I was missing work which equated to financial loss. I wouldn't have funds for the bills that were already drowning me. The idea of going back after I thought I was moving forward killed what was left of my spirit. I broke. I cried and hollered and asked God, "why?" We always ask why. We get into dry places in order to understand the source of the water; I needed to get back to the source. The truth is, I was in jail because I didn't pay my ticket. I had a habit of not completely finishing things that were important. I could not move on in my purpose if I couldn't handle facing important things head on. In addition, I cannot grow if my emotions speak louder than God's word. You can't do anything from a victim's perspective.

Did you know that you have to be broken from your unproductive thinking in order to have the proper mental foundation for what God has destined for you? You must unlearn the lies and misconceptions that have become your foundation and truly learn about God for yourself. There was a lot of trash in my thinking that was preventing me from trusting God the way I needed to. No matter what, if the pain eased up a little bit, I would get comfortable and fall back. Comfort is a contradiction to faith. God did not want me to be comfortable; he wanted me to grow. I did, too. I stopped my pity party and picked up a book by Bishop T.D. Jakes that talked about the pillars of faith and the whole armor of God.

We get our little communion outfit and kerchief and church hat and Jesus t-shirt and think we are equipped for battle. God's word says to put on the whole armor of God and then it proceeds to tell you what that armor is and what it protects: loins of truth, breastplate of righteousness, feet of peace, helmet of salvation, sword of the spirit, and praying always! That is how you prepare for battle. It has nothing to do with how strong you are and everything to do with all that God is. We are the light of the world; the salt of the earth. If we forget who we are, who can we help? When you allow yourself time to reflect with God, he brings you back to His word. You recognize your strength because you understand the immeasurable strength of God. What is in God is in me. When you lead, God needs you familiar with every level so you speak from a place of truth. Knowledge becomes wisdom. Faith becomes application. Battles become victories.

No matter what we see or feel, we must learn to trust God and his divine plan for our lives. God knew our end from the very beginning. The only person who is unaware is us. Until we make our communication with God our consistent top priority, we will not hear the direction he has for our lives. We will have to fall down seven times, to stand up eight, always knowing that, regardless of the number of times we fall, the number of times we stand will always be greater. Be willing to release what you think you know in exchange for the promises of God. When I focused on God, I was able to pray with and encourage the women in jail with me. I learned how strong I truly was and my testimony was a badge for the glory of God. From the valley, you see your way out, but only by looking up. The longer you focus your attention up, the quicker you will rise out of your situation. From the mountain top, you are reminded of where God brought you from, the beauty of all that he has created, and the infinite possibilities of being connected to an infinite God. I encourage you to keep your eyes on the hills, from whence cometh your help.

DR. JACKIE EVANS PHILLIPS

CHAPTER 5

Finding Ms. Lady

Jarmaine V. Lee

The happiest day of my life was the day I held her in my arms for the first time. It was amazing how our bond was so strong, Ms. Lady and I, from the beginning. She was sleeping when I arrived and still she felt my presence and settled in with a comfortability that is unexplainable. The love between us was so strong that I knew we would be able to endure the toughest of test this life had to throw our way. What I didn't know was that we were soon to cross that bridge and experience just how strong our bond truly was.

For the first month of her life, I was right there, feeding her, bathing her, putting her to sleep. I didn't do too many diapers because that wasn't my thing. It's funny because I would be trying to put her to sleep and she would put me to sleep first. Ms. Lady was always good at spoiling me and I thought that was my job. I'd say, "Give me a kiss, Ms. Lady," and she would start sucking her little baby lips and drooling! It was priceless!

I regret receiving advice that caused me to move away from her and her mom. I was promised that I could get a good paying job and move down South with the ability to get a house that would be my own in a matter of months. This offer seemed too good to pass up and so I jumped on it. Going against the wishes of her mom and even going against my heart, I jumped on a three-day bus trip down South. Ms. Lady cried the entire time that I was on the bus. But each time the bus stopped, she was asleep. She didn't want to eat, she wasn't trying to be held, and even giving her a bath wasn't working. She experienced this for the entire three-day journey.

By the time I made it to my destination, she was in full blown panic. I told her mom to put her on the phone.

"Ms. Lady, Ms. Lady, you have such strong lungs!" I said.

Upon hearing my voice, she began to calm down and started laughing. I heard her grandmother enter the room and ask what was done to calm her down and who was she on the phone with. It was me. Later on that night, I received a call saying the same thing. She would not stop crying. I began to sing the melody that I sang to her when she would lay in my arms.

"God has smiled on me! He has set me free! God has smiled on me. He's been good to me!"

Ms. Lady fell sound asleep!

My seasons were felt in my child. She knew that the winter was coming and that there would be a period of time that would test the bond that we shared. She was so right. About a month or two later, I had realized that I was brought down South under false pretenses and that none of what I had been promised was true. I was in a tough position of trying to make ends meet and finding a way back to my baby girl. She was the only thing keeping me going at this time and being away from her much longer than was anticipated was starting to take its toll on me. I was losing weight and sleeping less. My temper was getting shorter and my tolerance for nonsense was diminishing by the second.

I can never forget the day that my world seemed to stop and time became by worse enemy. I was speaking to Ms. Lady's mom and she wasn't in the best of moods. She had been disappointed that I had left and really didn't want to share with me everything that was going on with them. I could feel in my heart that things weren't right and it just felt like this was the last time we would talk. I didn't want to hang up the phone but the person that had convinced me to leave my family for all those false promises asked to speak on the phone. The next thing I knew, she was telling Ms. Lady's mom that if she didn't want to talk, then she didn't have to talk. I begged her not to hang up the phone. She did anyway, laughed in my face and told me that if I wanted to talk to her that bad, then I should have never left. Now I had come down South and we were currently staying in a hotel room with some truck driver who felt like he was the only man that needed to be in this room. Consequently, I was put out the next day. What I didn't know is that Ms. Lady and her mom were evicted at the same exact time. Talk about lightning striking in two places at once.

For the next several years, my life was filled with animosity towards those who had convinced me to leave as well as an inner hatred for myself for being so foolish that I would listen to two people that had proven to be selfish in every one of their choices throughout my lifetime. I was in a bad place of mind. I found myself adopting toxic behavior and mixing it with positive and inspiring people. It was an odd way of finding balance. I was incapacitated when it came to seeing pictures of Ms. Lady or speaking about her wellbeing. Not knowing was killing me softly through stress and partying. I had to find a better way to cope.

I began working multiple jobs and using every resource I could think of to try and track them down. I would pay for those internet resources that give you the last known address and then send you through several hoops and various payment plans that would give just enough information to piss you off. It was becoming unbearable. During this stage in my life, I am thankful that I had this good brother who was constantly praying with me and for my family and me. He knew how much Ms. Lady meant to me and how apologetic I was for ever leaving.

I ended up leaving the South and joining the United States Air Force. This was almost like a frequency gift for me. It assisted me in overcoming some of my issues with discipline and it put me in position to think about my predicament more clearly. It was in the military that I was able to set things in motion to eventually establish contact with Ms. Lady again. I did my technical training on the coast of Mississippi and this was just a few hours from where Ms. Lady's mom had grown up. Now the likelihood of them being in Mississippi was about as slim as a dollar bill but I had to at least take the chance. It was a Hail Mary for sure, but I was willing to take the chance.

For three months, I was faced with some type of hang-up. One week we had extra cleaning duty, on another few weeks we had the Special Olympics. I'd go to the rental car place and would be held back from getting the car on another week. Finally, it was coming to be my last weekend there before I was to be shipped off to my base in a completely different state, and we not only had extra duty, but we had a hurricane coming straight for us. I wouldn't be hindered by any of this!

I went A.W.O.L. from duty and rented the car without any issues at all. I drove to the hometown, following my heart and the Google maps! Once I got to the first exit, I jumped out at the nearest gas station and asked, "Does anyone know Ms. Lady's family?" A lady at the pump told me to go to the next exit up and make a left at the stop sign. I did just that and asked again. A response came back; they may be around the corner. I found a youth there who took me to the mall. While I was at the mall, I saw a woman with whom I shared a moment of familiarity. When the youth asked her if she knew Ms. Lady's mom, she replied, "Is it the Little Mother or the Big Mother?" I spoke up and said, "It's the Little Mother!" She then said "You're Ms. Lady's father!" I felt so overjoyed that someone had finally said my daughter's name to me! I knew that I was on the right course. She directed us to her aunt's restaurant and I was back in contact with Ms. Lady and her mom. This was one of the happiest days of my life.

Until it wasn't.

A short while later, the letters stopped coming in and we weren't talking any more. I didn't understand what was happening. It wasn't anything in me that would make me think that we would lose contact once again. I wasn't understanding. Then I received papers to appear in court for child support. I gladly went. I flew from the east coast to the west coast at Christmas time, just dreaming about the chance to see Ms. Lady again. To my surprise, they never showed up to court. I was pissed, but I would not allow this to be an end all for me. I had been in this valley for quite some time now and to have an opportunity to come out and have my daughter in my arms again was phenomenal.

I didn't have the letters that were sent to me. I only knew the street name. I wish I had committed it to memory but I hadn't. There were hundreds of apartments on this one strip of street. It was overwhelming. I would not be conquered though. I knocked on every single door until I found them. When I first laid eyes on this beautiful 2, almost 3-year-old version of me, I was star struck, just like I was when Whitney Houston had sung Happy Birthday to me at Red Lobster when I was a preteen.

Ms. Lady was so intelligent. She knew her colors and shapes and all of the Disney characters. She was very aware of her feelings when it came to me. Her mom introduced me as a friend, but I told her she knew who I was. I ended up getting on all fours and barking at her on the floor as she dug into her toy box. She immediately dropped her toys and came to me. She stood before me, forehead to forehead, nose to nose, and grabbed both of my ears and started barking back. What Ms. Lady did next gave my heart the sweetest joy. She hugged my neck and said, "I Love you, Daddy!" Talk about making a man melt!

Sadly, this season of our lives was short lived. Her mom got married not long afterwards and we got disconnected again. This was beginning to become a cancer in my life. After all I had gone through to find her, she was gone again. I was about to lose my mind up in here up in here! So, I began to express myself through poetry. I would perform all over the City of Chicago and all across the mid-West. I would take this opportunity to express my feelings for Ms. Lady and how much I miss her and love her. I'd talk about what life was like being homeless and striving for a better life. It all seemed so far away though. I could never seem to get stability and security with her missing. It was what seemed to be an impossible feat, just like having her in my life. However, I never gave up hope and I never quit trying to find my dear heart!

It was a snowy night in Chicago when we were closing our showcase out to a song my guy and I did to our daughters. I started the song out and began rhyming to Ms. Lady as if she were right in front of me. I expressed my grind and how hard I hustled to have her back in my life. Then the chorus dropped. Then, after the chorus, I was rhyming, but it was Ms. Lady's response to me! She told me that she was doing great in school and she had a lot of friends. She told me her mom was married and she was getting a baby brother soon and that she was very excited. Then the Chorus Dropped. I then closed with the joy I felt that she was doing well and that neither time nor distance could separate our love!

Two weeks later, my god-sister contacted my little sister and said that she was in class with Ms. Lady's mom and that everything that Ms. Lady had mentioned in my rhyme was true. Of course, sis didn't know about the show that Sunday night. It was just awesome that I was able to tap into Ms. Lady's frequency and then receive proof two weeks later. Although I still wasn't in a good place, I felt substantially better. Then, exactly one week later, I found out that I had a son and he was in the same town that I was in. This was crazy to me because I didn't even know about him, although I always wondered.

I began to build a relationship with my son, thinking in my heart that I would never allow what had happened with his sister happen with him. We've grown closer over the years and I have since then gotten married and found stability and security. But there has been this missing link. The void that had been in my heart for years was beginning to cause friction in my other relationships. I was unable to love my son completely because I was missing the love of Ms. Lady. I have always come close to finding her and things would seem to work against me every time.

My season didn't begin to change until I began to change my thought process. I was determined that all of the years of not having the resources that I needed to be there for Ms. Lady or my family would not cut it any longer. I determined in my heart that I would change myself in order to change my situation. That way, when Ms. Lady does come back this time, I will be prepared. I never really knew how to love until I said "I do" and got married. It was then that I could see that the pain of not having Ms. Lady in my life was impacting my wife and our sons. They all began to believe with me for the sake of their step-daughter and sister.

Then it happened: I found Ms. Lady on social media on her birthday. Two weeks later, we had the opportunity to speak online. Then things went silent once again. I wasn't discouraged this time. I knew that because my love for her was so strong, just like in *The Alchemist* by Paulo Coelho, the whole Universe is conspiring with me to get her back in my life. I set my determination and trusted that God would guide my steps and he has led me right back to her once again. Well, just the other day, I entered my summer season. Her mom called me and all of the pain and stress and anguish of all these years of not knowing and not seeing her have truly lifted from me. She was in the background talking to her mom and my spirit leaped from within me. Hearing Ms. Lady speak for the first time in 16 years since I heard her say she loved me has truly set my heart at ease.

I must say that the journey isn't over by a long shot; but the patience that was necessary to get this far was in so many ways divine and personal. There were moments that I knew that God had placed Angels in my life and along our paths; but there were moments that we had to tap in for ourselves. Everyone's Valley is different and they all present various obstacles and hurdles. Yours may not last as long as mine, and it just may last longer. The key is to not give up hope and to persevere in spite of what the situation may look like. Don't give up hope and know that all things are working together for your good! They did for me so they will for you as well!

BREAKTHROUGH

Sonya Weir

When your stories are old
And the truth is still untold,
Breakthrough.
When the preaching of the word
 Is not soul reaching anymore,
Breakthrough.
When you feel way out of touch
And his spirit you don't feel as much,
Breakthrough.
When your last miracle is aged
And your praise and worship seem staged,
Breakthrough.
When your heart don't have a song
And you feel you don't belong,
Breakthrough,
When in certain circumstance
You seem so distant and in trance,
Breakthrough.
When you don't pray like you should
And things don't happen as they could,
Breakthrough.
When you no longer fast
And you stay chained to your past,
Breakthrough.
When opportunities seem to pass
And you don't get because you don't ask,
Breakthrough.
When you can't take off your mask
And in His grace you cannot bask,
Breakthrough.

When you can no longer run in the race
And you can't keep with the pace,
Breakthrough.

CHAPTER 6

Set Back To Be Set Up

Madonna Lilburn-Thompson

*"YEA, THOUGH I WALK THROUGH THE VALLEY OF THE SHADOW OF
DEATH, I WILL FEAR NO EVIL: FOR THOU ART WITH ME…"*

-PSALM 23:4

This was a prayer in which I would seek a refuge, a shelter. It kept me, my mother, and grandmother in God's hands. I continue to say it throughout my life, hoping that it will bring the same comfort to my children and grandchildren. God is always there in that spiritual phrase.

As I think back, I identified the "valley" as the major separation from my common-law husband, leaving me to raise four young daughters on my own. I suffered from "solo parenting."

It was the year of the millennium. Of my four daughters, my youngest, Tiyah was only a year old. Never did I imagine I would raise these girls on my own. My dream was to raise my kids in a two-parent household, how I grew up. It felt like this was the beginning of a nightmare.

I constantly thought about how my parents would receive this devastating news. The prospect haunted me; I just could not allow them to witness me struggle with four kids by myself. Their thoughts and happiness meant a lot to me. Naturally, every child wants to make their parents proud. I felt as if I was a disappointment. One of the hardest things I had to do was sacrifice my single family home with the white picket fence, and settle for less. That was when my American dream was shattered. I did not want to be looking back, only to lose my future.

A CHILD WILL TAKE CARE OF YOU AND OUT-LIVE A HOUSE

Although my parent's house had plenty of space and I was welcome there, I chose to move in with my mother-in-law, Georgia Thompson in her single-family home. I called her Gee, for short. Practicing humility, I put aside my pride. It did not matter what people thought. I had to do what was in the best interest of my kids and me.

"THOUGH HE SLAY ME, YET WILL I TRUST IN HIM."

-JOB 13:15

It was difficult to explain to the children about the separation and moving in with Gee. They could barely process what was going on, but somehow had a lot of questions.

They were so young. Ishia was the oldest and nine years old. Following her were three-year-old Niyah, two-year-old Shaunae and one-year-old Tiyah. In our family, we often referred to the last three as "the girls" being so close in age. They were each a year apart, but there was a five-year gap between Ishia and Niyah.

From my perspective, Gee and I had a good relationship. We talked about things that would benefit the kids: work, current events, and life in general. Gee's house was the best living arrangement for my lifestyle. Her residence was literally down the street from my hair salon, making it convenient to get back and forth to work.

We lived in her single-family house with a den off the kitchen where the kids played and watched television. On that same floor was William Prince, Gee's father, whom we called Granddaddy. Beside his bedroom was Gee's room, along with a living room and bathroom.

Our huge upstairs bedroom had a big walk-in closet, with space for Ishia's twin size bedroom set. The girls had toddler beds and dressers. The room even fit my queen set. It must have been the size of half the house because it was above most of the downstairs rooms. Being close by allowed me to grow as a mother. I bonded with the kids, and was often present, which is necessary for kids of young ages. I was able to hear them when they woke up or needed me in the middle of the night.

Gee added another full bath for the girls in the basement. It seemed like Gee and Granddaddy gave us the run of the house. I cooked, cleaned, did our laundry, and grocery shopped on my days off while the kids were at school. Tiyah could hang out with me. Gee came home before us so most times she was in her room by the time we arrived. I tried to be as considerate as possible to Gee and Granddaddy by keeping the noise down. I immediately gave the kids baths as soon as we arrived home. On weekends, we were hardly there with me at work, the kids at my parents, and church on Sundays. Gee sometimes helped to get them ready for church. I didn't mind the help; I just didn't want my family to be a burden on anyone. We tried to give Gee space to enjoy some peace in her home. On Sunday we were away most of the day, coming home just in time for bed. We spent this time with my parents, ate dinner with them, and I even bathed the children before we left. Everything was close by, even the church, which was at the other end of Blue Hills Avenue, and my parents lived on a parallel street.

The salon, MADONNA'S HAIR THANG, was also located on Blue Hills Avenue in Hartford, Connecticut, in a busy commercial area. There was plenty of parking space around the building. It was above a West Indian restaurant and a corner store. Next door was a MR. PIZZA place, and the down the block, a Chinese restaurant.

The inside was spacious containing a waiting area with television and surround sound music, natural hardwood floors, large mirrors at the workstations, shampoo, dryer, and facial rooms. My sister, Debbie, worked providing facial and eyebrow waxing services around the times she attended hair dressing school. The waiting room was partly for nail service by technician Monica Jennings.

My daily routine was exhausting. I started by fixing the kids breakfast. Ishia got dressed and ate her breakfast in the car. First, I dropped her off at the elementary school in East Hartford. She wanted to remain in the same school she had been attending to be with her friends. I didn't want to disrupt her life any more than I already had. Next, I dropped off Niyah and Shaunae downtown at daycare. We listened to Disney kids' radio or played Eye Spy. I tried to make good use of the time we spent together to make learning fun. Tiyah, my youngest, was not old enough to attend so she went to my cousin's during the day. Her stop was last. I then went back home to get ready for work. I used my lunch break to pick up the girls from school. We did all of those things religiously. On Saturdays, they went to my parents until I was finished with work. Most times, my mother took them shopping with her, one of her hobbies.

I tried to make our Christmas budget similar to what the older girls were used to. I purchased a real Christmas tree. I have always enjoyed the smell of pine around the holidays. Gee and I would trim the tree and place it in the living room in front of the big window facing the street. I did Christmas shopping with my sister, Debbie. On Christmas Eve, I waited until the kids were asleep before I put their gifts under the tree. This was our tradition as if Santa came. Their father and I used to wrap the kids' toys and then lay their new clothing on the living room couches. Each person had her own section of new clothes.

Christmas Day arrived with the kids rushing downstairs. The first one down was an excited Ishia followed by a shouting Shaunae. The first thing that caught her eye was Ishia's life size stuffed animal. She jumped on the seat said, "Look at that big ole dog!"

with a raspy, still sleepy voice. and hugged it tight. As each came downstairs, Ishia took her to her area and helped each open her gifts. It brought me joy to see their reactions. Niyah was the last to wake up. When she did, they played all morning until it was time to make our holiday visits.

Although they were happy with their gifts, there was one thing I wished I had been able to get for them and it bothered me. With that thought, there was a knock on the door. It was my brother Ray and his wife Tamara bearing gifts. The girls unwrapped their gifts: coats! Exactly what I was concerned about! "God will give it to you if he can get it from you," a common expression, came true. The girls were very lucky to have aunts, uncles, and loving godparents. They showered the girls with love and gifts, on holidays and birthdays. All were part of our life to serve God's purpose. My father-in-law, Lionel, and his wife, Kitty, spoiled the girls with gifts that weren't in my budget. Annually, on Christmas night, all the grandchildren received matching pajama sets along with one expensive gift of their choosing.

Thompson Christmas tradition had the grandchildren spending the night at Lionel and Kitty's house. On other holidays, Gee's tradition was baking, coloring Easter eggs, and giving them money to buy what they wanted. My mother gave gifts like jewelry, underclothes, pajamas, dolls, and other things she thought they needed. Holidays were fun, even though it was one more thing to add to my busy life. The everyday running around back and forth was so exhausting.

One day, my sister-in-law, Sherrell, suggested I also drop off her kids in the mornings since Niyah and Shaunae attended the same daycare. My girls loved that because they got to be with their cousins. In exchange, Sherrell did the afternoon pick up for me. This meant I only had to get Ishia from her aunt's house where the bus dropped her off. Clearly, I lived by the phrase, "It takes a village to raise a child." On our ride to the salon, we conversed about Ishia's day. Eventually, Ishia progressed to where she needed time to practice her violin, recorder, and complete her homework. I dropped her at Gee's so she had no distractions from her sisters and this also gave her a head start preparing for the next day.

PRAYER KEEPS EYES ON GOD AND HAVING A NO-NONSENSE FATHER PLAYS AN IMPORTANT ROLE IN BUILDING ONE'S CHARACTER

It was during that period that I came into myself. I began setting short- and long-term goals.

"NO WEAPONS FORMED AGAINST ME SHALL PROSPER."

-ISAIAH 54:17

I felt a strong need to get back what I had lost. I dreaded hearing my father say, "You are going backwards," meaning you have lost things you have already acquired and you are not moving forward.

My long-term goal was to eliminate the running around. I wanted my salon close to home, either in the upstairs of a house or in a duplex, and to have a yard for the kids to play in. I recalled at the beginning of my journey that my brother-in-law was just expressing an opinion when he suggested I move to the projects. He was concerned that it might work to move in with Gee in case we didn't get along. I was offended. I now believe that it was this moment that served as a catalyst to push me to remain focused. It was the feeling of being underestimated that kept me motivated.

In order to reach short term goals, I knew there was going be some sacrificing immediately. I had to pay off everything I owed. Saving up money and cutting back on expenses was the only simple way I could achieve my goals. So, I stopped recreational shopping, and when I had to shop, it was only for necessities, birthdays, and holidays. This was difficult, so I just didn't go to the shopping mall in order to discipline myself. Most times I would even say no to going out.

"LOOKING AWAY FROM ALL DISTRACTIONS."

-HEBREWS 12:2

Occasionally, when I did go out, it was with the same "girls' night" group. I knew each person from different walks of life: family, such as my sister Debbie and sister-in-law Sherrell; friends like Lesa, Keisha, Camilla and Yolanda; or my companions from the salon, whom I socialized with even outside of work, like Melissa, Shan, and Monica.

I did not go out with my friends often; instead, I volunteered to babysit for the family. This meant that the kids had company, which always excited them. The girls' relationship with their cousins grew close as a result of being together so often, especially since they were so close in age. Spending time with my children was important to me.

HE WILL GIVE YOU DOUBLE FOR YOUR TROUBLE

Coming into the season of getting my dream was even better than I imagined. We moved into a single-family house in East Hartford with the salon next door. A tall, white fence in the backyard surrounded the fruit trees, and it had plenty of parking. God will give you the desires of your heart.

"AFTER YOU HAVE SUFFERED A LITTLE WHILE,"

-1 PETER 5:10.

The covering of the Lord was on my life; the girls remained at daycare downtown until Tiyah and Shaunae were old enough to attend elementary school in our town. Niyah graduated kindergarten that year.

Life became much easier with that move. The older two had buses to pick them up right on our street. I could watch them get off the bus in the afternoon right from my salon. They each earned Student of the Month throughout their elementary and middle school years. They expected to see me at their ceremonies so I scheduled my clients accordingly.

Eight years after the separation, Ishia graduated from high school and Anthony Thompson and I were married. The girls were so happy as they now had their dad around to take them to their basketball, soccer, and volleyball games. He planned his work schedule around the girls' sports; being a truck driver and owner made this possible. Niyah and Shaunae were both captains of their teams. Tiyah played on the basketball team all 4 years of high school and was awarded Most Improved Player. On weekends, they went shopping with their dad. He bought them phones, perfect timing for what they needed. We went to church as a family, and ate dinner together on Sundays.

Now the girls have all graduated from high school. Tony taught the girls how to drive and bought Ishia her first car upon her graduation. Ishia is enrolled in the AIR NATIONAL GUARD while also working in a group home with special needs individuals, and is furthering her education. She is independent, hard-working, and cares for herself. She is outgoing, a good friend, sister, and daughter. Ishia has a beautiful, intelligent daughter named Avery Rainell. Avery is an exceptional granddaughter. She is a one-year old who enjoys learning new things and retains information impeccably. I am honored to be one of her first teachers. She is truly a blessing from God.

My second child, Niyah, is working in a group home as well, part time, attends college for journalism, and is an aspiring model. She is independent, kind and caring, funny and enjoys traveling. Niyah's adventurous and spontaneous characteristics allow her to maintain her determination to become a broadcast journalist.

Shaunae graduated with honors from an international baccalaureate high school. She is currently enrolled in college full time where she studies to become a pediatrician. She is also an official airman enlisted in the AIR NATIONAL GUARD. She works part time as a department store manager. Presently, she is attending a technical college for her service-related duties. Shaunae is a strong, brave, thoughtful, and driven individual.

My baby girl, Tiyah, graduated as a high honor student from high school but with college credits. During her sophomore year of high school, she attended HARVARD UNIVERSITY in Cambridge, successfully passing college courses. She invented an application as a part of the LENOVO SCHOLAR NETWORK and was chosen to present it in California as a national winner. She missed out presenting because it conflicted with her summer classes which she felt came first. The following summer she was an intern at TRAVELERS INSURANCE COMPANY and received the Best Intern award.

In the summer of her senior year, she interned at BANK OF AMERICA, learning a lot that will help her financially navigate through life. She was so excited to share with us about managing credit and other financial advice. She is a full-time student at the UNIVERSITY OF CONNECTICUT studying political science. She became a sophomore mid-year of her first year of at UConn. I am proud of her hard work and artistic accomplishments. In her senior year, she drew a beautiful mural of black historians, containing subliminal messages. Displayed at her senior night award ceremony, it was also chosen to be displayed in the UConn magazine. Tiyah is a focused, disciplined, fun, adventurous person. She seems to have achieved a balanced life.

Thinking of the trials in my life, I now see it's been a set-back for a set-up to be elevated. This ordeal has served as an eye opener as to how God operates. When we invest in our children and push them further, the further we will all be.

OUR JOBS MAY BE OUR RESOURCE; GOD IS OUR SOURCE

Life is a fight and we just can't quit too early. We have to embrace the fight, for it will strengthen us for the next to come. God has answered my prayers. I have witnessed it manifest in our lives. We started off as a family and with God's help we will birth a nation of God-fearing people. Having good kids is not just a blessing; it's favor and grace. I humbly encourage you saints to remain faithful, and to have patience, even when it seems like our prayers aren't being answered. The Lord is a Way-maker, who made a way for me to raise my girls safely. I have remained a virtuous woman through it all. Thank you, Lord!

MY ALL I HAVE CONCLUDED

CHAPTER 7

Forgiveness

Monique Taylor

Forgiveness in the valley. Do you have enough faith to forgive and be forgiven? That is a question that seemed as if the answer was unclear, and so farfetched to me. It was the uncertainty of the answer that forced me to explore how forgiveness had me stifled in the valley. It wasn't until I learned how forgiveness works that I realized I was getting in my own way of getting to the other side. In my valley of forgiveness, I was harboring pain from the guilt of losing my family at the age of twenty-one.

I used to think that God didn't love me because he had taken my immediate family from me. My father, when I was in fifth grade; I was so young and I was daddy's little girl, I couldn't comprehend what I had done for my father to be gone at such a young age. Then, I went through losing my sister at the tender age of twelve years old; but in her death, I learned so much. She had touched so many people, from educators, to young people; she was truly a trailblazer in her own right. Then, I lost my mother at a pivotal time in my life. I had just graduated from college and was transitioning into the workplace when my mother was taken ill and then subsequently passed away.

I began to doubt that God loved me. How could he yet have me encounter all these hardships that seemed insurmountable? I doubted because I had lost so many people and felt that I was incapable of being loved. I had guarded my heart to ensure that I wouldn't be hurt again. I was BROKEN. It didn't matter how many people told me they loved me; the love of your biological parents is irreplaceable. I started to allow myself to accept temporary satisfaction. I did allow people into my life but there was a threshold that was impassable. There was a wall that I wouldn't allow to come down because I doubted that I was worthy.

Have you ever been in a desolate place where you didn't understand why you didn't believe? I had to look myself in the face and realize that I was worth fighting for and my love was valuable. I had to realize that my mother's mistakes were not my own. I had to realize that losing my family was not my fault but it was a part of my process.

Then, an awakening happened. It was as if God allowed me to look in to the mirror one day and said, "I'm going to use your pain to produce your purpose." Although I labeled this pain as being hurt, God used it to begin to heal my heart. I have since realized that forgiveness isn't always necessarily for the person being forgiven; it's about the process of healing that is activated in you when you release and let go. How could God forgive us when we make mistakes repeatedly, yet he still allows our lives to be blessed by his grace? I wanted to know how to forgive people who had hurt and abandoned me. The very first lesson God taught me was that it wasn't about me.

When we choose to operate without forgiveness, we allow ourselves to repeatedly stay stagnant in the same process, going through the same cycle because we haven't grasped what forgiveness is connected to. Forgiveness is wrapped up in freedom and liberation.

Have you been so bruised that you choose to not believe forgiveness can work? Have you gotten so buried by the circumstances and people who have hurt you that you don't believe in forgiveness? Are you choosing to allow your healing and freedom to be blocked by your own internal inhabitants of anger, resentment, and sadness?

Carrying the burden of un-forgiveness forces you to continue to suffer in sorrow and sadness. When you have gotten to the place where you have carried the burden too long, you acknowledge the pain and begin the process of healing. Forgiveness is a process that helps your healing begin. The act of forgiveness is one of those things that we must deal with to move through the valley and onto the next summit of our lives. If we keep holding onto old hurt, or carrying around a grudge, we only hurt and prevent ourselves from getting to the other side of the valley.

There is a powerful transformation that occurs when you are in the center of the valley. You are faced with a life-altering decision, to continue to allow the other person to have control over where God wants to take you, or not. For me, it was evident that forgiveness was my lifeline past the hurt. I could no longer carry the mistakes that weren't my own. My forgiveness is something I needed to accept and do, or I would continuously get stuck in the trauma, and emotional abandonment. Forgiveness forged liberation and freedom in my life to be unapologetically who God has called me to be.

Let's be clear. The act of forgiving those who have wrongfully hurt us doesn't mean we are condoning or excusing their actions towards us. True forgiveness is a willingness to let go and give yourself permission to move forward. It's the realization that you are stronger than that incident which can become a stumbling block in your life. Why not use the power and authority to forgive and then those stumbling blocks become your stepping stones out of your valley. Un-forgiveness has a way of keeping your mind captive where you cognitively feel that you can't cut the bonds of the past. Are you ready to release the temporary pain that has made you feel powerless? Are you ready to fulfill your purpose and help bring others out of the valley?

It is a beautiful thing to be able to take back your power. When you accept responsibility for your life, you give up excuses and begin your quest for freedom. Forgiveness brings a liberation that is indescribable. True forgiveness frees you from the contamination of your past. When you blame other people, you relinquish your power to them, but when you forgive them you are making a declaration that they no longer have the access or power to hurt you.

The day I decided to take my power back was the day I stopped being bitter. Those things and people who rejected me had held me hostage. I learned that forgiveness is a process and I couldn't begin it until I conceptualized that I needed to cut the cord. When we forgive, it does not minimize our pain or erase the scars we have endured. It simply allows us to move on, and begin again by letting go of the past, and pressing toward the future to live the life God has intended for us.

Today, I am willing to forgive those who have offended me. I will move forward in forgiveness so that I may heal. I acknowledge my scars, but I won't allow them to hinder my progress. I will live out the act of forgiveness daily, so that I may heal and help others on their healing journey through the valley. Daily, I will demonstrate love and joy. I will remind myself that forgiveness is my pathway to liberation.

GREATNESS WITHIN

Sonya Weir

Fear set in.
When friends and acquaintances
Speak of the greatness within
Within.
Within me?
How is it that I can't . . .
That I ain't see?
Ain't see the greatness within me.
Am I short sighted
Or is it the 'noise'
That might have drowned out
Drowned out the 'visionary' me?
'Unblinded', what might I see
What might I see
If the veil, unbroken veil
Was removed from within
Within my retina
Shedding light,
Light within
Within me?
Then I might see
A mirror,
A mirror image of yah
Greatness
Reflecting in me.

DR. JACKIE EVANS PHILLIPS

Extinguish your fears and live your dream."

-S. Weir

DR. JACKIE EVANS PHILLIPS

CHAPTER 8

The Fight

K. Stephen Wilson

I describe the valley as a place of low altitude. So low, the only place to look is up. You can hear life around you and even see the beautiful sky. But this place called the valley somehow grabbed a hold of me at a very young age. I was actually in 8th grade when this began. I felt the slow decline emotionally year after year and while I didn't foresee me in that place, I guess the events arrested my attention and life stood still. What was to come, no one could prepare me for. It wasn't supposed to end up this way. The valley also provided a space of healing and this is what I'd like to share with you.

It's late night/early morning and I'm lying in bed. I can't remember what took place the night before. I just remember waking up hearing my mother whimpering through the wall. This was strange as my mother was a strong woman. I also know she was a woman of faith and often would be up praying late, early, whenever "the spirit" bid her. This wasn't that type of whimpering though. Something was wrong. I nervously got out of bed and went into her room. As I entered the room, I could hear the whimpering more clearly.

"Mom, are you okay?" I asked her.

She replied, "No, my chest hurts."

I asked her if she wanted a cup of tea. Growing up in a Jamaican culture, tea, especially mint tea was the cure for everything. She agreed to the tea and I followed through. The tea seemed to ease her chest pain a little and she was able to go back to sleep. This chest pain would become more frequent and eventually led to a visit to the doctor. During the visit, they discovered a lump in my mother's chest. During the weeks to come while they tested the lump, worried conversations about the big "C" were being held. Up until this point, my mother had been fairly healthy. She was very active in the church, singing in the choir, baking for certain events, and, of course, providing what we needed at home. You see, she and Dad were married and complimented each other so well. Mom was the more outspoken one where Dad was very reserved but worked hard.

The results came back and it was not cancer. Surgery was required to remove the lump and that went well. Mom recovered and was back to work in no time.

"Son."

"Yes Mom."

"I have something to tell you."

Were we moving? Did she get another call from my teacher? I tried to beat her response with answers in my head until she said, "I found a lump in my breast." What did this mean? Was it the big "C" this time? Was she going to be ok? She took my hand and I touched it. It didn't feel normal at all. I felt like a ball.

"Mommy, does it hurt?"

"Yes," she replied. "I'm going to the doctor so they can check it out."

Mom went to the doctor and weeks later the test came back positive for cancer. This was the turning point of her health. She went through with surgery and they actually removed her left breast. She also had to undergo chemo therapy. Seeing her go through these physical changes such as hair and weight loss was scary. I wasn't used to her being sick. During this time, my father was very attentive and family and friends came to support around the house.

The road to recovery went well again and Mom soon regained her weight and grew her hair back. She had pretty much returned to her regular self. A year went by and life resumed with the family. It seemed like the worst was over and better days were ahead.

I moved from 8th grade into my freshman year of high school, which was pretty fun. I had older cousins who were there as well as friends from junior high. Socially, I had a blast exploring this new journey. It would be a matter of two years before we received word again that another lump was discovered in my mother's right breast and this too needed to be removed. This time, I didn't know what to think. Growing up in the church, in the Christian faith, we prayed and put our faith in God. I continued to pray and ask God to heal my mother and I believed that he would do it. My mother needed care after the third surgery as it was difficult for her to use her arms. She called me into the bathroom one day and said, "Look, son." She showed me that the two breasts had been removed. Her nurse then excused me from the bathroom as she washed up my mother.

Wow! Did this just happen? My mother, in her most vulnerable state, showed me what had taken place. She was still in good spirits though, which eased my concerns. She pushed through this transition and was back on chemo therapy. I remember going to a few of her appointments with her. On one of the last appointments, my father was with us. When we returned home, Mom couldn't get out of the car. She couldn't walk. She had lost strength in her legs. This was scary. What's crazy is that I don't remember her panicking. I remember my father going over to her side of the car and picking her up to bring her inside. This was the most heroic thing I'd ever seen my Dad do.

Things continued to decline once we got home. Soon, Mom needed a nurse at the house every day and she appeared to be getting weaker. It was at this moment that I began to decline in emotions. Worry set in and I wasn't sure what was going to happen. Many of her friends came to the house to pray and visit, attempting to lift her spirits. Soon Mom would be moved out of the house and into what was explained to me as a "Hospice." A what? What was a hospice? Where was this place? Why was she going there? No one explained why she was going there to me. Was she going to get better? I later would discover upon visiting that a hospice was a place where the terminally ill would be cared for until they passed away. At this stage, the cancer began to spread. I remember going to visit my mother as she began to get weaker and lose more weight. I couldn't focus in school. I couldn't focus at home. I remember my last time going to visit, my aunt was standing outside the door.

"Are you sure you want to go in?" she asked.

What? What did she mean if I was sure?

"Of course I'm sure," I replied and walked into the room.

To my astonishment, I quickly paused. I now was looking at my mother, eyes rolled in the back of her head and this breathing machine connected to her. This is what they meant when they say people are in comas and on life support. I had heard it, but never witnessed it. I saw her chest go up and down. After being startled, I quickly ran to her bedside and began weeping. This didn't look good. In the state she was in, it looked really bad. She had lost all of her hair and when I went to touch her head, I discovered a massive bump. A tumor had grown in her head and she had a big bulge in her chest. I began apologizing for everything over the years. I told her I loved her and just held her hand. I don't even know how long I sat there as the tears wouldn't stop flowing. I remember leaving the room because I couldn't take anymore and seeing a friend crying as well. I knew at this point that this was it. There was no coming back from this. We were losing my Mom.

As I left the Hospice, I slipped down a little further into the beginning stages of the valley. I remember this numb feeling coming over me and I didn't want to talk to anybody. I ended up failing a class and was actually in summer school during this time. I had explained to my teacher what was going on. The following day, I was still numb. I usually caught a ride with a very close friend. Once I got in the car, I just began to cry. My friend (who actually was my cousin's cousin so we called each other "cousin") asked what was wrong. I told her my Mom wasn't doing too well. As I got on the bus, I was usually very social, however on this day, I sat by myself and continued to cry. I remember a close friend asking if was I ok and me replying, "no." When I got to school, I couldn't focus in class. My teacher noticed something was wrong and asked me. I told her. I left school that day afraid of going home. I didn't have a good feeling the night before nor the entire day. When I got home, I received a phone call from my cousin that Mom had passed.

"Steve," she said.

I answered "Yes, Gerry." She went on to say "She didn't make it." I sobbed, "What do you mean?" She said plainly, "Your Mom died." In a state of disbelief, although I had expected it, I hung up the phone, hopped in the car and was on my way up to the hospice. I remember a family friend yelling, "Steve, don't go." What do you mean, don't go! This was my mother. I wanted to see her for myself. As I walked into the room, there was a still silence. There she lay, lifeless. I began crying again and gave her hug. This was it. Mom was gone.

After the funeral, people began to scatter out of our lives. I began to sink into the fullness of the valley, isolating myself in such a broken place. I became so angry at God because he was supposed to heal her. I remember driving on the highway and thinking about how I was going to drive off the bridge. At what point do I turn right? Would I make it off or just crash into the shoulder?

A few school friends invited me out one Friday and this began another coping process that became dangerous. I had smoked marijuana before but this was the most I'd ever smoked at one time. I also was introduced to alcohol. We were underage but there was this spot called the "bootlegger." All we needed was money and we could get liquor. These substances took away the pain. They made me feel better for the moment. It wasn't until one night I was driving home intoxicated and high that I remember seeing headlights coming at me and honking the horn. Oh no! Did I just almost hit someone? I don't even remember how I got home. I just remember stumbling down my stairs and making it to my room. I woke up the next morning trying to replay what had taken place. It was then that I realized I had hit the valley. I remember getting on my knees and crying out to God, asking for his forgiveness and begging him to help me out of this situation. I remember telling him that no one else was here. Everyone who said they'd be here, they weren't. I remember telling him that I really needed him.

After that morning, the climb out of the valley began. As the months passed, here was a peace that God had given me. I remember asking him why and hearing a voice say, "She belongs to me. I loaned her to you for a period of time." This helped to ease my pain. God got to me to the point of recovering and sobering me up so that I could see what was ahead. I wanted to graduate high school. I wanted to graduate college. I moved into my senior year broken but better. Each day was a new journey. I successfully completed the year and graduated. I recall lining up for graduation and realizing that my mother was not going to be there. I began crying once more and walking up to our seats was difficult. I remember singing with the class "I BELIEVE I CAN FLY." This was my break out and part of my healing. I had lost Mom, but I believed that I could still fly.

In my valley, I found despair. Desperate for a way out, I depended on people. I depended on substances. And while they eased my pain temporarily, there still was a vacancy, an uneasiness within. At my weakest and most vulnerable time in my life, God proved to be God. He provided strength. It's a strength you can't explain because, although you can't see him, you feel something pushing you, something bringing you joy where there was sorrow. My journey out of the valley took years but it made me a stronger person. The crushing produced wine and my message to you is to know that there is a way out of the valley. Your situation may be completely different from mine. But in the valley, we all experience a similar numbness and emotional barrenness. It's in those moments when man doesn't have the answer. Today your valley, tomorrow your victory!

I leave you with these words from a song by Cory Asbury:

There's no shadow you won't light up, mountain you won't climb up, coming after me. There's no wall you won't kick down, lie you won't tear down, coming after me. Oh the overwhelming, never ending, reckless love of God. Oh, it chases me down, fights till I'm found, leaves the 99. I couldn't earn it, I don't deserve it, still you give yourself away. Oh, overwhelming, never-ending, reckless love of God.

DR. JACKIE EVANS PHILLIPS

CHAPTER 9
Narcissistic Love

Sascia Hayden

Growing up, my family always told me this Jamaican proverb, *"NUH CARE HOW HOG TRY FI HIDE UNDA SHEEP WOOL, 'IM GRUNT ALWAYS BETRAY 'IM."* Translation: "It doesn't matter how much of a disguise someone puts on, their true self will always surface." This statement never seemed true until my relationship with Oscar.

Oscar and I met as teenagers and our paths crossed a few times over the years. At 31, our paths crossed again, and we decided to pursue a relationship. He presented himself as a responsible man on the surface and displayed the qualities I searched for in a partner. As the relationship progressed, he moved into my home; however, his true self began to show. His life was an illusion that I had fallen for. In doing so, I opened my life and world to him. Unfortunately, it allowed him to manipulate and control the relationship to his benefit.

It started with demands such as ending friendships with male friends I'd known for several years, to limiting or cutting communication with family members. Oscar's justification was, it would help our relationship. I didn't think much of it, but I agreed and did as he asked. This was the start of my poor decision-making that led to me losing myself and self-worth. It also started the emotional abuse that progressively got worse in the relationship.

The relationship was plagued with infidelity, where Oscar used an online dating profile to communicate with other women. When confronted with the evidence, he excused it as work-related. I rationalized that it could be possibly due to the nature of his job. But his behavior and actions proved otherwise. He stayed out late and did not return until the next day or several days later. Any plans we made were not a priority for him as he was either late, canceled plans, or didn't show up. He believed his explanations could compensate for his broken commitments. He also tried to buy my forgiveness with gifts or random dinners.

With each month that passed, not only were my emotions being abused, but so were my finances, mental health, and spiritual life. He manipulated my emotions and mind significantly that I made costly decisions which have impacted my finances. We outlined a plan to get rid of debt, manage household bills, and to save money. Unfortunately, this plan ended up being only one-sided. He saw the plan as an opportunity to utilize to his advantage. The plan of paying off debt, resulted in him maxing out my credit card and creating new debt. The plan of him being responsible for paying the household bills led to termination notices in the mail which I had to resolve. The plan for saving more money, led to me withdrawing money from a retirement account for him to use as a stake in a housing investment. This investment turned out to be but a con to seize my money. To stay afloat, I accepted a job for which I had no passion. Even with this new position, I could barely afford anything, and I had become dependent on Oscar for money to pay the bills and buy food. These poor decisions left me in significant debt, losing over twenty thousand dollars.

I hoped the relationship would be better and I convinced myself it would. However, his manipulation and lies increased, as did the abuse. He berated me with assertions that, not only made me weak but made me question who I was. His statements and abuse were consistent, to the point where I became isolated from friends and family. I was lost and did not know a way out or who to turn to.

When we met, I was nearing completion of my second Master's degree. However, over time, I lost my desire and drive to complete my work and eventually put school on hold. My interest in church became less, and when I did attend, I could not hear the message being told. The fundamental elements of a relationship were not present, but I was under his spell and was convinced that he loved me. I expressed my concerns to him and how the relationship was affecting me.

However, it had no impact on him or the situation. He told me I was a weak person. I was the one who needed help and should go to see a therapist. I thought things couldn't get any worse until the day he became injured in an accident and totaled my car. In his weakest moments, his true self was on display. While I was assisting him at home, he got angry and started to cry out for his mother. He left the house in pain, intoxicated on prescription medication, and drove his car to his mother's house for her to take care of him. I felt so worthless. I began crying and wondered, how could one person be so callous and heartless? I kept asking why.

Why am I allowing this to happen to me? Why am I so stupid? Why am I putting up with this? Why are you doing this? Why are you allowing this man to do this to you? I asked this of myself over and over. The answer was simple: I allowed it. I allowed a man who had no good intentions to do this to me. I allowed it because I was desperate, and I settled for the illusion he sold. I allowed it because I was in my thirties and I wanted marriage, children, and a family. I wanted all of this by 35, so I allowed this man to walk over me, lie, steal, cheat, and destroy me. I wanted to rush a process without proper guidance from my family and God. I lost sight of myself and my faith. I could not see or hear anyone, not even my God during this point of darkness.

During my darkest stage, the unexpected happened. My dear uncle passed away from cancer. The news left me numb and searching for comfort. Naturally, I expected consolation from Oscar; however, all I received was emptiness. My grieving period was lonely and empty, even with family and friends around for support. My uncle's death was truly sad and was a great loss; yet it was an awakening for me. His passing made me realize that life was precious, and I could not continue living this way. The relationship with Oscar had to end and I needed to regain control of my life. I informed Oscar the relationship must end. However, I was still grieving, and he managed to persuade me to stay. He stated he would work on improving himself and the relationship. It was yet another lie. He tried to buy my affections with gifts, but this tactic had no effect. He scheduled couples' counseling sessions thinking it would help our situation, but it only provided more evidence for ending the relationship. In desperation, he attempted a marriage proposal which I rejected. Again, I told him the relationship must end. Upon hearing this, his true self appeared once again. This time, he threatened my life because he was losing control over me. Due to this threat, I was advised to file a police report to get him out of my home.

Eliminating Oscar from my life and home was difficult but it was worth it. When I finally got him out of my home and life, I thought it was a time of new beginnings. Unfortunately, it was short-lived as I was served with a lawsuit from the car accident he had. Upon reading the suit, I was unsure what to do and how to approach it. I got on my knees and prayed to God for guidance and strength as I began this new journey. After my prayer, I had a sense of reassurance. I did not know what to do but, I decided not to be broken by this or any obstacle that appeared along the way. I saw an attorney who advised me what to do regarding the lawsuit. The lawsuit took almost a year to be resolved. There were times I was unsure if it would end in my favor. The one thing that was consistent during this time was my faith in God as I placed my burdens in his hands. I realized it was a year that God took me through. I decided to continue seeing the therapist from the couples' counseling sessions. I needed to address underlying issues which contributed to my behavior during the relationship.

I had to repair the mental and emotional damage that was done during the relationship. While seeing the therapist, I had to address each area of my life that was abused during the relationship: my finances, personal relationships, and spiritual relationship.

After Oscar, I had significant debt, a job I had no interest in, and I was living from paycheck to paycheck. I decided it was time for a change and I needed to work in a field I was passionate about. The process took several months with several rejects. With each rejection, I prayed and kept faith that God would lead me to the job that was right for me. When the timing was right, I was offered not one, but two job opportunities. I accepted one of the offers and began my new job in a field that I am passionate about, online learning development. Next, I created an action plan to reduce the debt accumulated from the relationship. I accepted my mistakes and decisions which contributed to my financial debt, but I would not be defeated or be defined by it.

While on my journey of healing, I had to address my relationships with my family and friends. I explained and apologized for any pain or hurt I had caused them. This was important, as I had to repair the damage created by my isolation and actions. With each change, I realized my spiritual relationship with God changed for the better. Not only did I attend church more, but I found a new sense of joy when I let the Spirit guide me and my decisions.

Many people may look at my experience and think this would never happen to them or they would never let that happen to them. However, there are many individuals who are struggling in relationships that are like mine, mistakenly thinking it is love. That is not love . . . love does not hurt nor cause pain. A loving relationship has respect, communication, honesty, trust, and most importantly, it has God at the heart of it. The experience from my relationship taught me the importance of patience, self-love, purpose, family, and faith. I've learned to never lose or undervalue myself; no relationship is worth being abused for.

As I continue my journey of healing, I am empowered with a purpose and passion to accomplish my goals, both past and present. One important lesson to learn from my situation is to never let obstacles stop you from accomplishing your goals and dreams. The impediment may be a setback and/or fear but use it as a motivator. I have used my relationship setback as a motivator to refocus on my goals, and now I have completed my Master's degree. Each day, I realize how much more I want to accomplish, and God provides opportunities when you least expect it.

I am passionate about designing and creating online learning modules. Therefore, I furthered my education in the field. While completing my degree and working full-time, I recognized my passion can accomplish my goal of being a business owner by 40 years of age. To finish my degree, I was required to submit a final project which I struggled with to find a good topic. However, God provided an opportunity in the most unexpected way from an old friend. As we conversed, I recognized I had two opportunities at hand. First, the ability to create an online learning module to assist my friend in his job, and the ability to submit my final project for my degree. Second, the ability to use this project as a portfolio sample and a launching pad for my business. This opportunity is one of many blessings in my journey of healing.

The more I continued to heal, more opportunities were presented to me. I crossed paths with Dr. Jacqueline Phillips, whom I had not seen since my early college years. I shared with her the recent events of my life and my journey to rebuild and move forward. She presented me with the opportunity to join her book academy and share my story in this book. At first, I thought my story was not as powerful nor impactful as others in the academy. However, as I wrote, I began to realize it was a healing process and it became an opportunity to share my story with other women. It is my way of encouraging other women not to settle or become desperate when the dream of marriage and family is not accomplished by a certain age. It is better to love oneself and be happy than to be with someone who will use and abuse you under the guise of love. My relationship was toxic and it blocked many of my blessings. To receive your designed blessings, you must remove any force that is blocking them. Each day presents new opportunities and new blessings. This is my motivator to remind me of who I am, that I am loved, and I can accomplish all the goals I set for myself. Someone may be walking a similar path as mine, so as the journey continues, take each step as I do with these two statements in mind:

"WE CAN MAKE OUR PLANS, BUT THE LORD DETERMINES OUR STEPS."
and,

"HUMBLE CALF SUCK DI MOST MILK." Translation: "Humility is more rewarding than arrogance."

DR. JACKIE EVANS PHILLIPS

"Anyone who gave you confidence, you owe them a lot."

-Truman Capote

DR. JACKIE EVANS PHILLIPS

HOW FAR IS HEAVEN

Sonya Weir

Disgruntled,
She found lyrics
That she affixed
To our situation
Of untold "bliss"
So in unison we yell,
How far is heaven?
Can you tell?
We are not
Content toiling in this hell
Though we dare not rebel.
So we questioned,
How far is heaven?
Can you tell?
We are toiling under a casted spell.
How far is heaven
I see no light.
My trust in God is my only delight.
How far is heaven?
Can you tell?
Heaven's now in my sight
So fare thee well.

DR. JACKIE EVANS PHILLIPS

CHAPTER 10

A Mother's Love

Reverend Matha Telca Ouellette

THE ONLY PERSON THAT DESERVES A SPECIAL PLACE IN YOUR LIFE IS SOMEONE THAT NEVER MADE YOU FEEL LIKE YOU WERE AN OPTION IN THEIRS. -SHANNAN L. ALDER

Blamed, cheated on, mortified, disrespected, verbally abused are few of the emotions I felt that propelled me away from my homeland. The scars of the abuse are deeply seated in my mind as a chronological memoir of my childhood days. In my St. Lucian culture, the idiom, "Time heals all wounds" is overused and misused. Friends and loved ones often tried to comfort me with these words; but their words of comfort never alleviated my feelings of pain and grief.

Transitioning from my homeland with two young children, thirteen and nine, was no easy decision to make, but I had no choice. I never wanted my kids to think that abuse in the home is normal. I never wanted my little girl to think that it was all right to have a relationship with a chauvinist, and my son to think it was acceptable to hurt a woman he supposedly loved. I was exhausted from the insults, the condescending accusations, and criticism. I had to make changes that would determine a healthy life for me and my kids.

I wondered how I would make my escape. The more I thought about it, the more difficult it became. I had to do the unthinkable, what I never wanted to do. Also, as the days came and went, I had sleepless nights just thinking of uprooting my kids from school, taking them away from family and friends. There were nights I struggled with my inner thoughts. It was like a wrestling match. I was envisioning myself fighting with my feelings by forcing them into painful positions or throwing them to the ground in defeat, just to erase them from my mind. My thoughts of escape bombarded me like a gust of wind almost crippling me or blowing me over like a tumbleweed.

Growing up as a child, I never saw any fights or heard of quarrels in my home except for the usual sibling rivalries. My mother and stepfather did their best in caring for me and my six siblings. Life as a child was not easy. There were times I wished I could have had the things that my neighbor's children had, the clothes, shoes, and even the toys they played with; but this was a little girl's fantasy. I wanted my children to experience all that was absent in my life. Reminiscing on my childhood days propelled me into desiring and seeking for a life of opulence for them. How would that become a reality? My thoughts again raced with great velocity, as I pondered. This was the moment of escape for me and my kids; the United States of America, a place of refuge.

It is humiliating to ask for help from siblings. This is something I never wanted to do, but in life things happen. Putting my pride aside was the ultimate thing I had to do if I wanted to get out of my misery. My siblings were clueless about my situation; all they saw was the material side of my life. Little did they know that life without love, happiness, or peace of mind was no life at all. Humbling myself to ask for monetary help was one of the hardiest things I had to do. I felt like time was running out, as I hastily picked up my telephone and made the call that eventually changed me and my children's lives. I called my sister in Connecticut and poured out my heart to her. Hearing my sorrows without hesitation, my sister gave me assurance and hope, promising financial help; this was music to my ears. My heart was filled with joy and when the night came, a sleepiness came over my body without any struggle, which was entirely outside of my control. The night swiftly went by as I awakened the next day.

In the afternoon, I received some cash from WESTERN UNION. I went to the travel agency to find out the cost of plane tickets only to find that the money I had received from my sister was not going to be able to cover all my expenses; but I was still filled with gratitude. Even though I didn't have the full amount, I activated my faith, made the reservation, and booked the flights for August 4, 2004. I silently breathed a word of prayer and left my situation in God's hands. I drove back to my home with my two kids, in utter silence, pondering how I would make up the balance for the tickets. Surprisingly, I had no fear of where the balance would come from; as a matter of fact, the surge of confidence raced up my spine and I felt energized and strong, believing in God to provide the balance. Disregarding my predicament, I felt that my struggle was about to terminate. My faith grew stronger and stronger as I prepared to put my kids to bed.

As I least expected, the morning arrived with illuminating sunshine. It was a beautiful day. My every breathing moment was, "How would I come up with the balance of the money?" As it is stated in James 2:4 (NKJV), "Faith without works is dead." I got into a trance-like mode and envisioned ways to earn or get that money. I made some telephone calls to my pastor and a very dear friend to make appointments to speak to them to ask for monetary help. Meeting with my pastor first was not encouraging. He felt my pain, but, he made me understand that, if he had the money that I needed, he would have no problem in giving it to me. But, since he didn't have the money, he had to bring the matter to the church board in giving me a loan. This was a place I gave my tithes, offering and time, but I was refused help in a diplomatic way. Hearing his rationale, the church board would think they were accomplices in helping me to leave my husband. I politely thanked him for his time and dismissed myself.

Plan "B" was already edging on my mind as I left his office. I called my friend and asked him to advance my meeting with him. I drove to his office, which was in the far north end of my island. Immediately after arriving at his office, I told him of my situation, trying my hardest in convincing him to loan me the money; but my effort was to no avail. He too thought that he would be helping me to separate from my husband and refused to lend me the money. There were no bad feelings; I understood and thanked him for accommodating and listening to me. I felt I was stuck between a rock and a hard place and wondered what my next move would be.

This was unlike my friend. It made me discern that God was using these disappointments as a strengthening factor in my life. In pondering all of this, I would become a better woman with a more vibrant faith. With this understanding, one would think my behavior would be different. I got to my home and hurriedly went to my bathroom. There I bawled and cried to God as if I was in agony, asking him to hear and supply the money for the plane tickets. As I prayed, my tears were like a broken reservoir gushing down my cheeks, and mucus running down my nostrils. I laid down on my bathroom floor pressing my palms on the mat, crying with a force, like a person vomiting on all fours. My kids were not at home, but if someone had to hear my cry, they would think that my guts were being ripped out. I pleaded with God not to forsake me but to answer my prayers. Knowing that the time was quickly approaching for my husband and kids to get home, I got up and washed my face, hoping that they would not recognize my swollen eyes. Leaving the bathroom, with excessive speed, I dashed into the kitchen to prepare dinner for my family.

While trying my best to compose myself and normalize my countenance, my telephone rang. With haste, I ran to the telephone, hurting my ankle in the process. Placing the receiver to my ear, I heard the voice of my friend at the other end. He apologized for turning me away and now wanted to offer me the money. With joy, I celebrated with a scream of elation, thanking him as if I was out of breath. In my last thank you, I heard the chattering of my children as they slammed the car door, racing toward the front door. With the ecstasy I felt, I could not conceal my happiness. It was all over my face. Finally, things were looking better. I had money for the plane tickets. The full total for the airfare was not realized, but I continued to believe in the God I serve for an uncommon blessing. With faith, trust, and confidence in my Lord, I was convinced that a miracle would have been birthed.

My next step was to purchase the plane tickets. There was a spring in my step as I went about doing my business with ease. The weight and stress that plagued my life began to dissipate little by little. The following day, I got out of bed early to get things ready for my kids to leave for school. After they left for school, I prepared myself and headed to the travel agency. On my way, I received a call from the airline agency saying that there was a special flight going to New York and the cost of our tickets were cut in half. This was the uncommon blessing I was waiting for. I was bewildered and overjoyed at the miracle God had done again.

Trying hard not to accelerate, I was there in minutes. I went into the airline office and paid the remainder for the three plane tickets. The money that was accumulated was a few dollars over what I had to pay for the tickets. Through the struggles in finding the money, God knew all the while the price I had to purchase the tickets. At that moment, I understood why God allows his children to go through the trials and testing of life. God made me understand that in our struggles, He is testing our loyalty, faithfulness, and our devotion to Him. Our flight was scheduled for August 4, 2004, which was the next day.

I drove home in haste, and on arriving home, I laid down three empty suitcases and began to pack our belongings. Moving from closet to closet and drawer to drawer, I placed clothes and important documents in the suitcases. It seemed like an eternity spent doing this, but I meticulously folded each garment, laying them neatly in each suitcase. Exhaustion got hold of me as I was moving from my room to my kids' rooms. Ignoring my exhaustion, I loaded enough clothes for each of us. Finally, as the evening drew near, our bags were packed and ready to go.

The next day at the crack of dawn, I was out of bed; the day of our departure was upon us. My emotions were all over the place. For a moment, I experienced happiness. This was short-lived followed by a wave of sadness engulfing my entire being. The thoughts of leaving my homeland, family, and friends, caught up with me and tears streamed down my cheeks unbidden. Fear flooded my heart, thinking of the uncertainty that awaited us on the other side of the globe. I mustered my strength and pulled myself together, purposing in my heart never to return to the clutches of my husband. Leaving my homeland was very painful, but even with this, I pledged never to step my foot on it again. Bitterness had resided in me for so long that I promised myself, whatever lies ahead on the other side would not cause me to return.

The time swiftly approached for me and my kids to leave, to embark on our unknown journey. Leaving the portals of my house, I received a barrage of verbal abuse from my husband, abuse that was loaded with profanity. Thankfully, my kids had no understanding of what was spewing out of his mouth. His action was intentional; he spoke in the vernacular of my homeland. In their innocence, they were excited to leave, knowing they were about to be on an aircraft. I, on the other hand, was choking on my tears, not wanting my kids to see my vulnerability. My husband refused to take us to the airport, so a dear friend was willing to drive us there. It was on the way to the airport I made two calls letting my elder sister and a girlfriend of mine know of my decision and my exit from St. Lucia. We got to the airport and in a matter of minutes we were airborne and on our way to the United States of America.

The uncertainty of the unknown fueled my anxiety as my kids chattered with enthusiasm and giggles. Questions flooded my mind intermittently as the pilot made his first announcement to make sure everyone was buckled up and assured us of a safe flight. I became more apprehensive as I looked out of the window; the runway zoomed by and the buildings got smaller and smaller as the plane gained altitude and began gliding through the clouds. There was no turning back. I quietly said my last goodbye as the kids sat in their seats, enjoying the ride. The flight seemed as an eternity, but we arrived and disembarked at J F KENNEDY AIRPORT. Our passports were stamped, our luggage cleared and was wheeled into my sister's vehicle, on our way to Connecticut. Three and a half hours *were an informal donkey's years*, since we had never driven so long on one trip in our homeland. We finally arrived at what we would call home.

Getting up at 2:00pm in the afternoon was a life-changing experience. The incredible mode of transportation, the huge sky scrapers, and all the people walking going about their business made me very anxious to bring up my children in this environment. I bounced back into reality and remembered we were here to stay. Though it was a culture shock, my children and I quickly tried our hardest to adjust to our new surroundings. The transition posed many difficulties for them. My sister, with a great deal of effort, tried to make our lives comfortable. My kids were registered in school, my daughter attended EAST HARTFORD HIGH SCHOOL and my son attended HOCKANUM ELEMENTARY SCHOOL.

My kids are introverted and attending school in East Hartford was challenging. My daughter cried every day during school because moving from classroom to classroom was not the norm for her, coming from a small island like St. Lucia. It was not long before the teachers noticed her struggles and they assigned a student to assist her. My son, on the other hand, never expressed his difficulties, but as a mother I knew he encountered difficulties daily. The time came when they both settled in and were able to maneuver in their new school setting. Time went by at lightning speed to when they both graduated high school.

Both my son and daughter, who were exceptional children, went to a two-year community college. My daughter continued at SAINT JOSEPH UNIVERSITY and graduated with high honors with her bachelor's degree in Human Biology, whereas my son took some time off from college with the intention to return later to complete his studies in Aero-engineering. The challenges my daughter encountered were overwhelming. Some of her problems were irrepressible. For instance, a letter was sent out by the university administration, stating that the college fees were being raised due to the high financial responsibility of the college. Hearing the news was like a nail in the coffin, an unavoidable stumbling block, but with God as my help, I refused to collapse under such attack. I paid the college a visit and laid out my financial dilemma to the head of the financial department. Again, God carried me through the valley with great favor from the college. Connie was able to continue her studies as I continued to pay what I was able to from the start. For my daughter, who was undocumented, her college life was a miracle. Her school fees were paid out of my pocket, and at the completion of her studies, she had no expenses or added expenses. The day finally arrived when she graduated with high honors and her tuition was paid in full.

These financial experiences brought me to the lowest point where I was financially depleted. But there is one thing we all can be sure of; God is always at work when we are at some crossroads in our lives. When we are faced with the trials and tribulation of life, when we are at a point of *not* knowing what to do, we can always trust and depend on God, because his word says,

". . . HE WILL NEVER LEAVE YOU NOR FORSAKE YOU" -DEUTERONOMY 31:6C (NKJV).

We all go through valley experiences in our lives; valley experiences are part of life. The valley experiences are ways to propel us into our destiny or purpose. Our attitudes in our valleys determine our blessings or curses.

It was at the beginning of my daughter's second year at PALMER COLLEGE OF CHIROPRACTIC when she felt everything was going as planned. Her tuition, apartment, utilities bills, car insurance, and every other basic need were being met and paid for. Then, the enemy, with sniper stealth, slid into the picture with a modified rifle and infiltrated her domain. She felt her dream of becoming a doctor start to crumble. My daughter's world was falling apart when I heard her voice on the other end of the cellphone. I envisioned her clenched fist, not knowing what to do. She was crying like a woman in travail; her screams were suffocating her every breath. Again, I visualized my child pulling her hair out, folding her hands around her belly as she screamed saying, "Mommy, Mommy, the bank sent a letter stating that I have reached my maximum and could no longer disburse money for my college tuition."

Hearing this had me feeling contractions as if I was having a second round of giving birth to her. I choked back my tears and got in warrior attitude and began to pray. I reminded God of the age I promised to follow him. I jogged his memory, telling him of my faithfulness and commitment to him. Also, I evoked his senses saying to him, "I have never turned away from you." I was filled with indignation as I expressed myself to the Lord. Getting up from my chair, I could see my tears on my cheeks like the trace of a slug on a leaf or like rain on a dusty window pane. It was painful to hear my daughter's cries and I wished I could have embraced her and let the torrent of her tears soak through my blouse. I wanted to stroke her hair to relieve her of her anguish.

It was King David in *PSALMS 23:4* who spoke of a deep, dark valley, where there seems to be no rays of light. In that valley, dead-end streets, disappointments, frustrations, and disasters are unending. As I journeyed through my valley, I kept in mind that God's grace, his leading, and his tender mercy will never fail. In the Psalms, David classified all these as shadows. Nevertheless, valley experiences can be the route to the Promised Land. Going through the Promised Land, there is no ultimate route or detour. Therefore, in our valleys, there are no ways to go around them. But, God has promised a way out to go through our valleys. Remember, David stated at the beginning of Psalms 23, "The Lord is my Shepherd." Shepherds lead and take care of their sheep. Valleys are temporary; they are not our permanent dwelling place.

After many days of praying and fasting, God did come through and gave me my break-through. He showed and advised me on ways to come up with the tuition for every semester. With a weekly pay of $600.00 and all the other ways of coming up with the finances, I was able to defray the expense of my daughter's remaining years at college; from asking, borrowing, and working hard to accumulate the funds for every quarter that was remaining.

During those difficult times, God miraculously sent angels into my life. My present pastor was one of these angels who lent me money from the church treasury. It was humiliating to go to the pastor for help but I mustered the strength and asked for the loan.

I will not sin, nor commit a felon, but will do everything in my power to take care of my children. My pastor, hearing my daughter's dilemma, assisted me, and for this I am grateful. Another angel was a church brother, who gave a loan for one month's payment for the rent, for this too I am thankful. In these grueling and arduous times, I fell in love with a good man. Hearing my struggles, he stepped in as a good Samaritan, voluntarily rendering aid for my daughter's college fees.

God has been a powerful navigator in my struggles, and my kids and I are not victims anymore, but VICTORS. In our flight to achieve what we now have, although it is not much, we did not commit any felony, or do anything that would compromise our faith. I was tempted to do what everyone does, to get an easy way out. Many people offered their help, but it was not God's will for our lives. We struggled. People whom I thought were my friends, whom I trusted, spoke ill about us. But we persevered, refusing to do what many are doing. My children and I kept our faith in, and our eyes on the Lord, and turned down every offer that would jeopardize our relationship with HIM. We will continue to walk the narrow path until we are self-actualized by the grace of God. I realized that God's hand was upon all that I and my children went through, and His timing is right. His grace and mercy have kept us, and with faith as our fuel, we will overcome.
I am determining to rise to the remaining path of the 'V' in the "VALLEY."

(Rom. 8:28 NIV) And we know that, in all things, God works for the good of those who love him, who have been called according to his purpose.

Our mess has now turned into a message. Our test is now our testimony. My daughter is now a practicing Chiropractic doctor in the United States of America!

CHAPTER 11
The Power Of Forgiveness
Alanna Chambers

As I sat in front of my grandparents' store waiting for my dad, I wondered if he would show up, or what he'd use for an excuse this time? I had been disappointed more times than I cared to remember. I loved him so much, and gave him so many chances. Much to the dismay of my mother, who'd dress me in my Sunday best, put on a positive face and give me pleasant affirmations, he often would not show up. Each time, I cried uncontrollably. Mom offered solace by buying me my favorite flavor from the ice-cream man who rode a bike selling house to house. She made excuses for Dad, assuring me he would be there next time. Repeatedly this happened. Occasionally, when he did pick me up, the trip was not child-friendly. I simply rode along for what he planned with his friends for that day, including watching him play cricket all day, or follow him while he went bar hopping. I would have to sit in a corner while he entertained his friends. Eventually, he stopped coming altogether since he and Mom got into disputes regarding his inconsistency.

My stepfather came into my life when I was six. I grew up in an extended family, surrounded by my grandparents, aunts, and uncles. My childhood was wonderful and surrounded by love. My grandparents adored me. Mom became pregnant with my sister and moved to live with my stepfather. My own dad became even more distant and unsupportive. Mom would have to go to the sugar estate where he worked on payday to obtain any support from him. The situation became so frustrating for my mother that she sent me to live with my father to ensure he took care of me. However, my father decided to immigrate to the United States. My mom thought this meant my father would have the ability to provide more support to afford me a better life. She was wrong; he forgot about his children he had left in Jamaica. He rarely sent money to my stepmother, who I was still living with, since the house was close to my primary school. My stepmother had one boy younger than me from my father, and an older girl, who was not my dad's. Soon, she started treating me poorly and taking out her aggravation on me for my dad not sending money. I told my mom, and she retrieved me to live with her and my stepdad.

My father exited my life. The patterns continued. Mom would have to go to my stepmom to ask for his latest address in the United States, since he was not corresponding with me nor sending money for my support. My stepfather told Mom not to ask my father for any money to support me since it was not forthcoming. I was fortunate enough to have the school bus to take me to primary school and bring me home. I was now twelve years old and going for my Common Entrance exam; passing this is required to attend high school. Otherwise, I would have to attend secondary school. High schools have more advanced curricula, a higher standard of education, and are usually private. Secondary schools are public education and less prestigious. I passed the Common Entrance examination for a high school in another parish. To attend that school required two bus transfers and a taxi, or for me to board with someone in that parish. Mom was able to find my father, who sent the initial school fees for me to attend the high school. He also paid for me to board in the parish. Soon, though, finances dried up, and I could no longer afford to board in the parish. So now I needed to travel back and forth to school. The commute was quite long for a young student; I was often late for school and could not stay for extracurricular activities.

I lived with my mother and stepfather, who had to take on the responsibility of getting me to school; the tuition equates to college fees in the United States, in addition to the cost of commuting. Mom obtained support from my grandfather, who reluctantly gave it since he felt that my father should be able to provide for me. I made good grades. I joined the RED CROSS, KEY CLUB and was on the debate team. I even was privileged to meet the Honorable Portia Simpson, then-Prime Minister of Jamaica.

LOSS OF INNOCENCE

Mom, at this point, had two more children and was now a stay-at home mom. There were four children in the house, so my stepdad was now solely responsible for me. We were happy for a while. We had family dinners and played games and enjoyed fun activities. Mom rented out one room to make ends meet. As I matured, I noticed my stepdad began looking at me differently. My stepfather has been in my life since I was six years old and had bathed me and brushed my hair; I viewed him as my adopted father. He became overly friendly with me and tried to hang out with me and my girlfriends to the point that I felt uncomfortable. I remember very vividly when going to bed how he pretended to tuck me in but actually was touching my intimate areas. I threw his hands off! He apologized, saying it was accidental. He saw my reaction and now re-strategized his next attack. I woke up out of a sound sleep to find his hands under my nightgown. After refusing his advances, I told him I was going to tell my mom. He started crying, begging me not to tell. I began going to my grandparents to sleep there. But Mom wanted me to come home.

My stepdad became more emboldened. I awoke to find him climbing on top of me while he was undressed and aroused. I was so scared, I ran to Mom's room. I slept with her the entire night – he had to sleep in the couch. I then started locking my room door, which he convinced my mom to disallow. He was more aggressive and started telling me that he would no longer support me if I did not do what he wanted. If I were to tell my mom, he would cut her off as well.

In my 12-year-old mind, I was terrified and did not know what to do; I had no one to talk to. It was too much for me to handle. I lay awake at night after my extensive homework assignments. Then I had to get up early to start my commute at 5:00am in order to arrive at school on time. It was torture; my grades were falling. One night, I could not keep my eyes open, I was too exhausted. I was awakened by him trying to rape me while threatening me that if I were to tell my mother it would hurt her even if she believed me at all. I was between a rock and a hard place. I had to leave; I had to escape, I could not deal with this any longer. I blamed my mother; I hated her for bringing this person into my world. I felt I had to run away.

I was now entering the crucial years of my high school career. I needed to board near my school in order to succeed. I appealed to my stepmom to intercede with my father to obtain funding. She was able to get me a roommate, and I boarded near my school for the remainder of the year. I was back on track.

My aunt then went to a parish where her husband was attending the university and teaching. I boarded with her for two years until they immigrated overseas. I was still in high school but there was no way I was going back to live with my mother and stepfather. I appealed to my grandfather who helped me with my boarding fees for that year. However, I had one more year left and did not have the resources. My best friend was living with her sister, whose husband was a teacher at my high school and lived close to it. She asked if I could live with her. This saved my final, most critical year where I had to take the cumulative exams, administered by the Caribbean Examinations Council, to progress to the sixth form, enter college, or find employment.

After high school, I lived with my grandparents. By then I was not speaking to my mother or stepfather and claimed that my grandparents were actually my parents. I knew I was on my own. The town was supported by a sugar cane factory where everyone worked. My grandfather had several acres of property where he planted sugar cane and sold it to the factory. He had a farm with vegetation and animals. My grandparents fed the entire community and hired half of them to help in his fields. My grandparents also had a grocery store and a bicycle parts store. I helped in their store. I worked at the sugar cane factory office as the general manager's secretary over the summer. I had to get out of this town; this was not the life for me. I wanted more. My grandmother had a progressive thinking acquaintance who was my only friend. She had several daughters in Kingston. Although I also had aunts in Kingston, I did not want to live with any family members. I asked my friend to persuade her daughter to allow me to live with her. She agreed. I packed my bags and left. I later immigrated to England and then to the United States. I was still not speaking with my mother.

THE POWER OF FORGIVENESS

As soon as I landed in the United States, my goal was to attend college. My dad was attending law school and living in New York. He was not prepared to have a teenage daughter living with him. I arrived in the winter; he gave me a light jacket. I was living in a boarding house with no heat. I contracted bronchitis. My aunt, who lived in Queens, had to come rescue me and take me to a doctor. I did not like living in New York, so I found a roommate and moved to Connecticut. By this time, my stepfather had immigrated to the United States and had abandoned my mom and his kids. I knew she needed my help; however, I did not want to think about the events of the past and certainly was not ready to forgive her.

I soon found work that paid for my education. I obtained my bachelor's degree then obtained two master's degrees. I later purchased my own home. My aunts implored me to take Mom to live with me. I prayed about it and soon she was in the United

States. I did not know her anymore and found it hard to relate to her.

One day, I sat her down and told her all that happened to me and how I resented her. She said she did not know of my terrible experiences at the hands of my stepfather. She assured me that if she had known, she would have left him. She cried. I cried. And in that space, we both found the power of forgiveness.

UNBROKEN ENIGMA

Sonya Weir

Consumed with what...what
I assumed...I assumed
That you and you predicted doom
I assumed...
That you, you and you predicted
That, I may never bloom
But I, am too black to crack
So I refused to lay back and die
No lie...
Reason why! I am now Consumed with 'try'
I refused to lay back and die.
I, refused to assume defeat
Though no easy feat I refused to lay back and die So I
applied...
My energy, my "know how" NOW...
'Cause I know why
I can't lay back and die. So I tried, I tried,
I took advice from The wise, sometimes.
I thread so carefully
As I refused to admit defeat
Refused to lay back and die
So I attack the stigma That's attached to me... Me?
Enigmatic!
I chose to be, 'cos
I know that, I know that
I can be that 'somebodee'
If I thread so carefully
Allowing these "harden" feet

To walk my destiny

As I refused to lay back and die.
And when my paean is read
You, you, you and you would have
Remembered all you had said, that

I; opprobrium...now
Stigma broken
I have spoken…
I "still refuse" to lay back and Die.

CHAPTER 12

Smooth Criminal

James Black

"I worry, I weigh three times my body I worry, I throw my fear around But this morning There's a calm I can't explain The rock candy's melted, only diamonds now remain, oh."

- John Mayer -Clarity

I swung and swayed in the stock room as I issued stock, intermittently grumpy, so much so that Maureen Harriot had to ask if I had prayed that morning. It jolted me! I thought long and hard about it and penned a song. John Mayer's "Clarity" still oozed its way out of the make shift speakers made by the former stock clerk. All the cashiers at the Inland Revenue Department had received everything needed to increase the government's coffers for the day. I was right to let the good times roll. Before any reflective process could begin, a worried-looking supervisor came in and asked that I go to her superior's office; no time was to be wasted. Being cavalier, I waited till the end of "I don't trust myself with loving you," another favorite of mine from Mayer. The good part of the song hadn't come around when the panic washed supervisor, usually a show of stoic repose, barked at me to hurry to some place I would rather not be.

Prancing like the pink panther, I skipped long-armed and -legged to the office, while half of Kingston and St. Andrew were queued up to pay taxes. My usual cheer was ineffective, reflected by the pale looking manager. So naïve was I that I missed the "hit team" that was sent to arrest me. I chuckled loudly, expressing my fascination with the military grade guns that they were armed with. So certain was I that there was some other fool named

James that was to be whisked away, I prodded further, hoping a smile would escape the five men fully clothed with instruments of death.

The manager bargained with them that I not be dragged through the foyer in handcuffs, while my rights were being read and a sound warning given, "If you make a run for it, you will be shot, if not killed." My face, now effused with a wide grim grin, waited patiently for Ashton Kutcher to jump from behind the counter to yodel, "PUNKED."

Between the office scene and the rear seat of the war-torn Pajero sport utility, I was at a loss. The M16's muzzle pointed to my face, the unmarked Toyota Corolla cars that went before and after the Pajero made me realize I was clearly Jamaica's Most Wanted! But why? A warrant was never shown to me. The bumpy roads of Kingston and St. Andrew almost had me forget the lump in my throat, that eerie feeling of uncertainty. Was this another test? Was this a joke? Where were the hidden cameras? I had already gone before the church for sexual sin, survived death and deadly rumors. What now was this?

The abrasive officers sped erratically to my house. They had to ransack my home in search of missing documents. I was piecing together the story as I sifted through the insults and curse words. I remained calm. The fellow to my left with the high-powered rifle was laced with slow moving beads of sweat. The men in the row before me argued liberally about women, music, and politics. The driver was stoic as was the gentleman in the passenger seat, who was well built, washed with lack of sleep and red eyes, and who busied himself in deep thought, entertaining the other gentlemen intermittently.

All three vehicles belched as their tires screeched in the cul-de-sac where I lived, as if to parade the intensity of their mission. This was a good movie in the making, with the script being written on the fly. God must have known that today was the day for my test as he showed up to me in subtle ways. First, the manager asked that I not be harassed; then Pauline White, a lecturer, surrogate mother, and woman of God, happened to be home on this incongruently sunny day.

A few years earlier, I had given my life to Christ, expecting a magical light to light from heaven to enshroud me in its spiritual mysteries. My soul was secure but the critical guidance I needed for right now was lacking. Tests and trials then came aplenty. I was young, wild, and with a propensity for getting into trouble. My mother and I were separated countries apart. I floated around, searching for meaning and a place to truly call home. The first home I found was Havenhill Independent Baptist Church on Mannings Hill Road in St. Andrew Parish, Kingston, Jamaica. Many saw something in me and reached out. I was far too raw and rough to be tempered, even with their best intentions. Even with speed bumps, there were great periods of growth, where I served in varying ministries by the power of God. It seemed though, that through all this, there were a few thorns in my flesh that would not budge.

As my personal battle with my flesh waged, God provided a home. Lisa Leslie, a friend, spoke with Damien Francis, son of Pauline White, who now ambled curiously out to the cul-de-sac to see what all the ruckus was about, my staying with them so as to attend church. Her eyes now wide as the distance between Kingston, Jamaica and Bloomfield, Connecticut, studied the impressive weaponry that now escorted me into my adopted home. As any concerned mother would, native to their instincts, she rushed to my aid, all while interrogating the officers, some masked. She was cordial and calm, as she always was, under dire circumstances, save some petty thing were to happen where she would blow all her fuses. The Glendale Place of Safety, as we aptly called her welcoming home, was now under the auspices of the law.

Questions tore at me as the well-armed men ripped through my bureau. My chest never once heaved as I believed this had to be God's plan. As the men grew more insulting, I recalled the words of the Apostle Paul who reassured,

"And the peace of God, which passeth all understanding shall guard your hearts and minds through Christ Jesus."-Philippians 4:7

The officers never found the documents they sought. The lead officer was puzzled; something was amiss. Again, I was neatly packaged into the back of the battle-scarred Pajero with gun muzzles for company. Again, I was berated for being a criminal, party to a ring of criminals who illegally peddled government documents, largely to other criminals. I calmly responded as the fire raged. I could hear an indistinct voice on the phone as the lead officer melted into subordination with frustrated and aggressive undertones. The phone was thrust at me and I was accused of criminal activities, how I must have "burned all the pertinent documents" that would have led to a sure end for "criminals" like me, and was advised that if I did not quickly admit guilt, I would be dearly sorry.

No longer wanting to suffer my insolence, I was shipped to the command center, where the worst of the worst criminals are interrogated. This is not a fairytale place where coffee is served and a mythical one phone call was allowed. I have heard stories through the grapevine of the hospitalized and of those who are no more, those who were dragged through these walls. Thankfully, Sister Pauline White was in tow. I prayed she would hurry and not be in one of her more studious pursuits that took an infuriating eternity.

The building was decrepit, a perfect hub for criminals. My doom was spelled out by the gentleman who logged in my name; as he fiercely held the book, I signed. I was chained in a corner to a cold metal bench and some pipes. Every so often a large, unhappy, dark as a grape black man would pass me by, decorating my ears with the more colorful of Jamaican curse words. He let me know I was "getting it," whatever "it" was. This madness was intermitted by a calmer, well-dressed officer who gently prodded at me to admit my guilt so that I wouldn't "get it," whatever "it" was. The hours rolled by; the discomfort was softened by John Mayer's rendition of Michael Jackson's "Human Nature," a favorite of mine. I also knew someone would have to play "Smooth Criminal." I chuckled loudly enough for the Hymenaeus and Alexander-like officer, large and dark, who sought to torture me as did the aforementioned wicked men tortured the Apostle Paul.

The aggressor motioned towards me, asking that my shoes, laces, and belt be removed; that I be taken to "get it." No sooner had his cruel face gleamed at the idea than Pauline White and Damien Francis come churning in. "To be absent from the body is to be present with my Lord."-2 Corinthians 5:8, I recalled, before they alighted on the scene. There was no time for niceties. "Just in the nick of time," was the only line I could think of. My loudest accuser was sorely aggrieved. I was chucked into an office, where the good cop, bad cop tactic was employed to "prove" my guilt. I endured this for hours on end. The room was so dark, I knew not where the sun lay in the sky. Ms. White's protestations could be heard faintly in the distance, contending for me.

Having made no headway for hours, as I calmly proclaimed my innocence, I was finally taken to where "it" was to happen, a wide office, much larger than the one I was in. The man behind the desk had more girth than the desk itself. He was infamous for his methods of reducing the most harrowing gangsters to helpless babes. I was unmoved outwardly, but a measure of fear slunk its way down my spine. After a few minutes of prodding and Ms. White's presence, refusing to leave my side though being asked to leave, the giant said, "I do not think you are innocent, nor do I think you are guilty based on the evidence before me. But hear this, the next time you come in front of me will be the last time you come in front of me. Get out!" Before any relief could wash over my face, the accuser who so taxed my soul, clamoring for the worst to befall me, wailed and moaned and went to retrieve more items to try to incriminate me. He was hell-bent that I was in collusion with those selling driver's license documents and other motor vehicle documents, raking in millions and should not be released.

The argument waxed on for some time. However, I was eventually released. I marched over to the head office where the voice on the phone was. An argument blazed as I poured out my vehemence. Soon I discovered that the valley I was in was not false accusation, not the threat upon my life, but the failure to see the face of God, his provision, his mercy, his infinite wisdom and guiding hand throughout my life and in this specific situation. As my temper raged at the executive powers that failed to come to my aid, and railed at the man, the voice behind the phone call, already there was waiting three women of God, in the executive meeting of twelve who upheld my innocence as I was being detained.

"Woe is me, for I am undone!"-Isaiah 6:5

"My brethren, count it all joy when ye fall into divers temptations;
Knowing this, that the trying of your faith worketh patience."
James 1:2-3

CHAPTER 13

Look Up. Love Never Fails

Seanna M. Bowen

Have you ever stubbed a toe so badly that the nail falls off? Usually, a new one grows in its place. That new toenail is symbolic of me, who I am, and the journey it took for me to become the woman I am today. I have found myself bruised and damaged. It was not before I totally shed the negative thoughts, actions, and influences of my past that I was able to fully manifest who I was designed to be. I had to free myself from toxic relationships, associations, and thoughts in order to grow. I had to heal my inner feminine spirit by forgiving my mother for the times she let her own pain morph into becoming mine. Throughout all these transitions, I have come to recognize the power of my own Valley.

I was born in Kingston, Jamaica in what was considered a middleclass upbringing. I knew what poverty looked like as it was all around me, but I never had to worry about food, shelter, or material comforts. I grew up as an only child, never having to share my toys or space with any siblings. As far as I knew, my father left when I was two years old and, was living in the United States. He would come home once a year for three weeks at a time. I remember the first time he returned. It was Christmastime and he brought back so many toys and clothes with him. I was five and the first in my neighborhood to own a brand new Nintendo gaming system. I was elated and the envy of many friends in the neighborhood. Simultaneously, I acquired many new friends as a result. As the years progressed, I became accustomed to my father being away for most of the year, but returning with many gifts annually.

As I approached the age of ten, I began to long for his constant presence. I envied my friends whose dads were with them. I grew jealous of seeing other children being picked up by their fathers and resented that I had to take the bus home. When I learned to ride a bike, it was my god-father who taught me. When I started a new school and part of the uniform included a tie, it was a male family friend who taught me how to tie it. In my teens, it was another male family friend who taught me how to drive. Whenever my family came to visit from the United States, I was jealous that my cousins had their fathers in their lives. I longed for the mundane activities that encompassed a normal parent-child relationship.

It was not until I was approaching twelve years old that I fully understood the nature of my parent's relationship. I recall a moment when I heard my father speaking to my mother about my older sister of whom I was previously unaware. I then asked them who that person was. My mother was very angry and immediately shut me down, telling me that I was out of order for interrupting their conversation. My father reacted differently. He told me the truth. I learned at that point that I had three older siblings from a different mother. I found out later on that he was still married and living with his first wife. Suddenly, everything made sense. I finally understood why I could only see him once a year.

Simultaneously, my relationship with my mother grew even more strained. As a latchkey kid, I remember being home alone in the evenings before my mother came home from work. I enjoyed the quiet solitude. Once she got home, I went to bed early, sometimes without dinner, just to avoid seeing her. She had a very vexing and contentious spirit. She found tasks for me to do and I could never seem to please her. It seems no one could.

I witnessed the dynamics between Mom and my grandmother and observed how my mother yelled at her whenever she went to spend time at her house. There was a deep-seated resentment that I just could not understand then. My grandmother retreated to her bedroom in silence to read her Bible. My grandmother was very dear to me. She read me stories from the Bible, and taught me how to truly pray. She provided the foundation for my faith. She also taught me what strength and resilience actually were. She told me the story of how she came to meet my grandfather and eventually became the primary breadwinner of the family by selling bananas on the side of the road, and doing the laundry of a wealthy white family. My grandfather was very likeable, but also an alcoholic. My grandmother remained very bitter towards him, even long after his death.

It was later on that I was able to connect the dots and recognize that my mother became the caretaker of the household. She was the middle child of five siblings. Her eldest sister had gone off at a young age and was married with her own family. Her older and only brother was revered by their parents and his responsibilities were few. If there was only enough money to send one child to school, he was the favored one, so she would stay at home. She was left with the duty of caring for her two younger siblings, as well as doing all the cooking and household chores. Later on, I learned that well into her adulthood, she carried the resentment of having to shoulder the family's burden. I understood that my mother was unable to love me the way a mother should. She has never once told me that she loved me. She lacked tenderness and care, as she herself had gone without. She was unable to be what she did not know how to be. I vowed that I would never become like her, and I would never deny my children what I was denied.

When I was seventeen, I got news that I would be living with my father and his wife in the United States. At first when I arrived in the States, I was adamant that I would remain in New York with my mother's sister and her family. Work was easy to find as I was lucky enough to land a position as a nurse's aide for a few weeks when I had visited a year prior. I was not even looking for a job but was glad to find one as I was able to buy what I liked and go wherever I wanted. I liked the hustle and bustle of city life and dragged my feet when it was time for me to go to Connecticut. My father threatened me, saying that if I was going to stay in New York he would not help me to pay for school. I was both nervous and apprehensive about the decision, but I knew I would have to live in Connecticut if I wanted to go to college.

I had met my father's wife when I was twelve years old. She was a decent and upstanding woman, and had allowed me to stay with them one summer when I was twelve. I had absolutely nothing bad to say about her. She went above and beyond to make sure my stay was comfortable. I learned later on from my own step-mother that my father told her about my existence when I was eight years old. She had had strong suspicions over the years, but did not know for certain until he revealed it to her. She had every reason to shun me but she was the one who initiated my immigration petition. She welcomed me into the fold but at first, the rest of my family members did not do so willingly. I was never openly disrespected to my face but behind my back, I was subject to false allegations and accusations. I discussed my feelings with my father and let him know how hurt I felt but he never once stood up for me, instead saying I should ignore them. I felt truly alone and depressed. I made friends at school and had a somewhat active social life. But beyond that, I was very unhappy and felt like an unwanted stranger in my family.

The next stage of my life was marked by a tumultuous marriage for eleven years. In addition, both my Dad and stepmother died during that period. During that time, I relied heavily on my mother. My relationship with my mother suffered greatly because I leaned too heavily on her. It sounds strange to say that a daughter, only child of a mother, leaned too heavily on her own mother. It does not feel foreign to me because as I grew to learn who I was and why I went through the things that I did, I also saw myself as an extension of my mother's void in her own life. When I called upon her to support me while I was going through my difficulties, I could not understand at the time that I was just asking her to do more than she was capable of. With the clarity and perspective that I have gained since then, I am more aware of why she responded to me the way she did.

My mother lacked compassion from her own mother, who likely lacked compassion from her own mother as well, and so the cycle continued. I recall once when I was rushed to the hospital and had a life-saving emergency surgery. The next morning when I was coming out of the anesthesia, my mother called the hospital and was connected to where I was staying in the recovery room. Instead of asking me how I was feeling, she asked what I expected her to do. In my partially sedated state, the only response I could muster in my confusion and bewilderment was that I expected nothing. She never called after that or visited to see how I was doing after that. I decided from very early on that I did not want to be that kind of mother to my own children. I had to teach myself to love them in a way that I have never been loved before. I had to see them in a light that I had not previously seen myself in. They were treasures. They are destined to be powerful women. They are children of God.

My faith in God helped me to overcome the difficulties of rebuilding my life after our divorce. We were married for eleven years and produced two beautiful children; he left us with a beautiful home. From my struggles, I have learned to harness every bad situation and turn it around for good. My favorite scripture is Romans 8:28 which says that *"all things work together for good to them that love God."* I was learning how to live my life for the first time as an adult without my parents' help, or without the security of a man's last name attached to mine. But instead, to lean totally on God and to trust Him throughout everything. It was difficult but I have never been disappointed because God is in the midst of everything *(Deut. 7:21)* and He is always right on time *(Eccl. 3:11).*

I cannot view this portion of my life with regret as it fueled me to step in the right direction. I was able to pursue ventures of which I never even dreamed of engaging. I became a radio personality and over a period of four years, I was on the airwaves in Connecticut, Toronto, Maryland, Miami, and Kingston, Jamaica. I did a brief stint on television. I wrote articles for various websites. I dabbled in promotions and entertainment between the United States and Jamaica. I met various celebrities throughout my brief tenure in the field. I was also the marketing director for a popular Jamaican beverage brand. After a few years, I decided to leave it all behind and do something I always wanted to do. This was to pursue a Master's Degree in Clinical Counseling and eventually my Doctoral degree in Neuropsychology.

Learning how to forgive is so important for a breakthrough in life. First, we must learn to forgive ourselves, and then others. By forgiving my mother, I was able to understand why she made the decisions she did. I was able to understand why my mother could not love me the way I needed her to. I forgave my ex-husband as well because I realize he was just a product of a toxic familial cycle. If I were to examine every failed relationship I have had, the same could be said about each person. My father was no exception. I forgave him because if it were not for him, I would never have been where I am now, nor able to see the other party's perspective. Forgiveness is essential to heal and to grow.

The strongest piece of advice that I have taken away from all this is to show love. Love yourself, and love others. I had to learn how to love myself. I recognize myself as a woman of strength, independence, and intelligence. I am beautiful both inside and out. Because I love myself, I also am obligated to show love to others. My stepmother did this for me as she accepted me into her home as part of her family. While she was on her deathbed and comatose, I kissed her forehead and thanked her for everything she had done for me. It is in loving others that we see the beauty of who we are and what life has to offer. I learned to love my mother from a distance until we could communicate without strain. It still remains a challenge but because of the love I have for my mother, I am able to see her through a different lens and to not take her abrasive nature as being equivalent to not loving me. It is through love that I send out into the world, with every person whom I come into contact with, that I remain confident that I will one day receive the kind of love I deserve. Love never fails.

LIVE
Sonya Weir

Live without excuses
    -have no regrets
Live with a purpose
    -display passion
Live a life of expectancy
 -be accepting to change
Live grateful
    -nothing is guaranteed
Live a life in the now
    -yesterday is gone and
Tomorrow is not promised
Be willing and ready
    -Stand armed
    -Stand alert

CHAPTER 14

Reconnection, Restoration And Rebirth
Crystal L. Hamer

"When you want to make God laugh, tell Him about your plans." - Woody Allen

It was February 2008. My friend, the sister of my high school ex-boyfriend, passed away from cancer. She and I had remained friends long after her brother and I broke up. In her eyes, I was the one who got away; the one her brother should have married. So, it was only fitting for him to honor his big sister's wishes by approaching me during the repast, in a hospitable, Atlanta gentleman kind of way. He had to make up for lost time, over 20 years, in that very moment because he wasn't going to let me get away twice.

After a 2-3-month courtship, which included an array of phone calls and visits to his home, he began to start talking about marriage. I was all for it since I wanted to move down South anyway. The bonus was, I would be making this move with someone that I already knew. Plus, my Middle Grades English teaching certification was expiring the end of June 2008. The timing seemed perfect.

So, he began planning a Bahamian cruise wedding while I looked for a teaching job in Atlanta. We were planning a future together. Most importantly, everything was going according to OUR plan.

Then, God stepped in with HIS Plan. I had no idea that He would take me through a deep, dense valley that would eventually restore me, rebirth me, and reconnect me with family. Most importantly, this journey through the valley brought me closer to Him. There's no way I would have the relationship that I have with Him now if I hadn't.

By the beginning of the summer of 2008, the time I was supposed to move to Atlanta, OUR plan went totally awry. First, my soon to-be husband's entire demeanor, vibe, and commitment changed completely, to the point where he was unrecognizable. He went from picking out wedding rings and preparing his home for me, to changing the code to his answering machine and not communicating with me at all.

Looking back, those were signs and ways that my ex was telling me that he didn't want to move forward with OUR plan, despite what he told me. I was just in a state of denial, in shock, and caught up in the fairy tale to fully see and accept it. Packing up a house and long-distance job searching further clouded my vision.

I never married him. Instead, I moved in with my Aunt Norvell and Uncle Van. I had reconnected with them when I thought I would be getting married and moving to Georgia. My aunt and father are brother and sister. My parents divorced when I was five years old and my brother, Ty, was a year old. After the divorce, we lost touch with my Dad's side of the family for several years. However, my conscience would not allow me to move to a state where I knew I had family and not reach out to them.

My Aunt Norvell and Uncle Van lived in Lawrenceville, Georgia, about an hour away from where I thought I was moving to. When I went to visit them, they suggested that I apply to the school district in their town. Ironically, my uncle said if I got hired, I could stay with them during the week and go home to my fiancé on the weekends. Little did I know that I would be moving in with them a couple of months later.

I had already packed up my home in Connecticut and rented it out because of OUR plans. Despite OUR plans not working out, MY new plan was to move forward with staying in Atlanta and making a life for myself there. I stayed for four months, living off unemployment checks and the kindness of Aunt Norvell and

Uncle Van. I had several interviews and offers there, but none of them felt right.

Those four months in Atlanta were bittersweet. I was extremely grateful to reconnect with family, but emotionally, I was at the lowest point of my life. I cried, questioned myself and God, and really prayed a lot. Aunt Norvell, a true child of God, counseled me and prayed for me. She also helped me with my resume and my cooking skills. My Uncle Van really stepped in and took on the role of a father. His knowledge base is like no one that I've ever met. Any subject that you want to know about, he can tell you. He is also musically inclined and extremely comical.

My cousin, Robin, also taught me about God's provision during that time. She and I had many Bible Study conversations. She shared the story of Job with me and said that, even though I was going through the valley now, God would restore what was taken from me, and then some, if I just remained faithful and obedient to Him. I was Job. I remember her telling me that I must stay focused and not let distractions and obstacles throw me off track from what God had in store for me.

My best friend, Shellie, was and is my rock. If God were a person on earth, she would be Shellie. We've known each other since kindergarten. Shellie is the epitome of Agape love. She is the only person that knows how to instantly assess a situation that I'm going through and help me through it. Whether it's checking me, calming me down, letting me vent, or just laughing until we are crying, she definitely is vital to my growth and development. During my time in the valley, she was pregnant with her son, Wesley. Yet, she was still there for me completely. I often look back at that time and think about how selfish I was. I really should have been focusing more on her and Wesley instead of myself. When you are in the valley, though, it's all about survival. You have tunnel vision.

There were so many people who helped me in different ways during my time in the valley through prayer, words of encouragement, recommendations, referrals, and tough love.

I remained faithful and obedient. It was very difficult, though. I read the Bible more and more to understand how God works and what His promises are.

By December 2008, things started to get better. I was beginning my trek out of the valley. It happened quickly in the beginning. My Uncle Van told me that it would and that I would get a job that I applied for in Glassboro, New Jersey. He cited some Equal Opportunity Employment laws as the reason why. Looking back, I know it was all because of God. Uncle Van was right. In January 2009, I started my dream job as the Director of Curriculum & Instruction with a Department of Labor contractor that operated several Job Corps centers across the country.

I stayed with that contractor, Horizons Youth Services, for almost nine years. Just like in Atlanta, I had family in South Jersey, too. As a matter of fact, my mother's side of the family grew up and lived in Bridgeton, 45 minutes away from Glassboro. When I first moved to Bridgeton, I even rented my cousins' house. Phyllis and Malcolm are my cousin Robin's sister and brother-and-law. It was a blessing to be surrounded by family. Another cousin, Tammy, Robin and Phyllis' sister, lived around the corner. On Saturday mornings, I would go to her house for her famous pancakes. I started attending church with another cousin, Denise, who is Robin, Phyllis and Tammy's first cousin. I continued reading the Bible, along with self-help and inspirational books.

During my time in New Jersey, I met a man named Clarence. We dated for four years. In April 2012, we found out we were pregnant. A few weeks later, tests revealed we were having a baby boy. I always wanted my first born to be a boy so that he could protect his younger sister when I had her. I was nervous and happy at the same time. Although Clarence and I had fun together and liked a lot of the same things, we were not equally yoked. I didn't want to bring an innocent child into anything less than a consistently, unconditionally loving and peaceful environment; our son deserved that much and more, and my pregnancy was high-risk. At the same time, I knew that a baby is a blessing, and at age 44, my biological time clock was on a serious countdown.

I named our son Cameron Tyler. We craved McDonald's French fries and vanilla soft serve ice cream. On August 1, 2012, I had a miscarriage at 17 weeks. I didn't know what was happening when the miscarriage started. I was in Albany, Georgia, at the Turner Job Corps Center, in the middle of a presentation when I began having sharp pains. I sat down and finished the presentation. Then, my water broke. The pains got worse; it felt like my abdomen was being twisted. I was rushed to the local hospital where I was admitted and discharged two days later. Before the nurse handed him to me, she said, "He is perfect. 10 fingers and 10 toes." He looked just like me with Clarence's clef chin and perfectly pointed nose. More importantly, he looked peaceful.

We were devastated when we lost Cameron.

Before the miscarriage, I had been trying to move back to Connecticut for about five years. After unsuccessfully renting my house out to two different tenants, I asked my boss on several occasions if I could work remotely from home in Connecticut when I wasn't traveling to the Job Corps centers roughly two weeks per month. It didn't make sense to me to pay rent in New Jersey and mortgage in Connecticut when I was traveling most of the time. Each time I asked, he said no. When I found out I was pregnant, I knew that I would have to discuss the topic of moving back to Connecticut again with him. I already knew that I wanted to raise him in my home and which bedroom would be his Lion King themed nursery. MY plan was to have that discussion with my boss the Monday I got back from my monitoring trip in Albany, Georgia. Instead, I had to tell him about my miscarriage from my hospital bed.

Finally, in August 2016, I was able to come back home to Connecticut. I was offered and accepted a Grade 7 and 8 English Language Arts teaching position with a charter school in Hartford.

Now, I am back in my home; back with my renewed Middle Grades English teaching certification and a charter school certification; back in communication with my Dad (who passed away March 26, 2018) and his side of the family; and back in a church that I was visiting before I left for Atlanta; however, I am a member now.

In addition, I have started a new business, The Cameron Tyler Network, which specializes in customized curriculum design and proofreading services. This is my way of resurrecting my son via two skill sets I'm tremendously passionate about.

God restored everything I left in June 2008.

I know this is my second chance, a redo to do things the right way, the only way, God's way.

According to His Plan.

"Success will ultimately come to you when your dreams become bigger than your excuses."

CHAPTER 15
Do It Now
Kimberly Gordon

It was a hot summer night and I was twisting and turning in my bed. I had so many things on my mind and on my daily agenda to accomplish. However, the thieves of productivity namely fear, doubt, procrastination and stagnancy, kept me bound and unable to make a move. I spent month after month listening to sermons from some of my favorite preachers. I listened to Dr. Cindy Trimm, how Deborah broke glass ceilings and how I should invest in myself. Pastor Tamara Bennett taught me the importance of the Holy Ghost. I listened to Pastor Micahn Carter who encouraged me to be more like Jesus. I remembered Pastor Larry Gunter's sermon on growing in the midst of discomfort, like the eagles. I listened to Pastor Steven Furtick who reminded me that there are three habits to a healthy heart and life. Pastor Charles Galbreath taught me about holistic healing in every area of my life. Bishop TD Jakes taught me that I should soar, and that God doesn't make chairs; he makes trees. Mel Robbins taught me to get up and launch into the life I want. But I just couldn't. Dr. Brene Brown reminded me that I should dare greatly and be willing to be brave and bare all in transparency and vulnerability, even if it means standing alone. Iyanla Vanzant taught me the importance of standing in the truth of who I am at all costs, and Oprah warned me to remind people to be responsible for the energy they bring into my space. Yet, with all these reminders and encouragement, I just couldn't find my breakthrough. All the positivity in the world is null and void unless we apply it to our lives. I was not lacking inspiration, encouragement, or positivity, but I was lacking the boldness to act and do it now.

I've heard time and time again during the course of my life that I should learn the lessons from life's tragedies. I remember always shaking my head and uttering the words, "yes" and "amen" in agreement towards this statement. I agreed with this statement mainly because life was good and the lessons were manageable. What happens when the lesson defies everything you ever believed? What happens when the lesson is a constant source of pain, sadness, loss and suffering? What happens then? I'm still trying to decipher the answers to those questions.

In December of 2014, for the first time in almost a decade, my entire immediate family was in the same physical space together. The family decided to spend Christmas in Georgia with the matriarch of the family, my beautiful and giving momma. My sister, Sherrie and I began talking about how our eldest sister was stressed out and needed a break. My eldest sister is a powerful single mother of three boys and she was going through a lot at the time. My baby sis, Sherrie and I began putting all the plans in place to make this trip a reality. We called my dad and his wife and asked them to come and be with the family for the Christmas and New Year's holiday in Georgia.

Things started going awry and it looked like this family get-together would never happen. But God, it was the most exhilarating and inspiring, fun time I had in my life. We laughed, talked, prayed, sang, talked, danced, argued, ate, talked, and loved on each other from 2014 into 2015. We shared our goals and dreams with each other. We listened to my nephews as they shared their feelings and experiences in school and out of school. We gave hugs, kisses, advice, tickles and then we said goodbye as we went to our various destinations of New York, Florida, California, and Connecticut.

Unbeknownst to us, that would be the last time that we would all be together in the same space on this earth ever again. Do it Now! In March of 2015, I received a phone call from my sister-friend, my ride or die, my baby sis. She was at work. I said hello and with her charming voice she said, "Hi, Kim." I said "Hi Sherr. What's up? How's your day?" She responded in the most peaceful and surrendered voice:

"So I have something to tell you. I went to the gyn the other day and I had a painful pap smear exam. The doctor found a cyst on my ovaries."

She continued to say, "The tumor is the size of a grapefruit and they are recommending chemotherapy. I went to the doctor to get it tested for cancer and, yeah, it's a tumor. Yup, I have cancer."

I honestly don't remember what I said to her, but I know my thought was it reached me. It's in my home. Now it's personal. I kept saying to her, "I'll research some natural remedies and maybe it's not cancer. Maybe it's a cyst that they can remove so you could be okay." I remember saying to her that "God is going to heal you. He has too much to do through your life to take you now! You're only 33." She told me that she got a word from the Lord saying that it's not unto death. After she told me that, I was sure that she was going to be healed and live a cancer-free life. I just knew God was going to heal her and get all the glory.

The Bible reminds me that his ways are not our ways and his thoughts are not our thoughts. It appeared that she was doing better, getting stronger and was approaching remission. Unfortunately, she began getting worse and her health began to fail rapidly. Her body was weak, but her spirit was strong. She remained to be the powerhouse, dynamic and spunky human-being we know and love. I referred to this period of my life as my new normal. My new normal was now my new reality and things would never be the same again. As I pondered on the words my 33-year old baby sister told me, "I have cancer," time stood still. My eyes were dry, but my heart was full. I looked at the walls, on the ceilings, in my hands, and then I shut my eyes. She continued to say, "The doctors are recommending that I get a hysterectomy and remove my left ovary."

As if things couldn't get any worse, between the months of March and April of 2015, we found out that she had Stage 4 bilateral ovarian cancer. Stage 4 translated to me as, "Ok, God, now is your chance. You can get all the glory by healing her and making her your living miracle." The idea of being on the earth without my sister-friend was inconceivable to me. The idea of not watching her marry the man that God designed for her to be with was inconceivable. The very thought of not traveling with her, not sleeping in our mother's bed on Thanksgiving and Christmas holiday, having family vacations and meals together without her was too hard to bear. The thought of my sister not being present to be my maid of honor at my wedding was unimaginable. My siblings, my nephews, and my parents would have to live with the reality that every May 5th until the day they die, would mark a day of grief and loss. It would be a reminder that Sherrie is not here; and we will never see her again.

My baby sister and I communicated extensively while she was alive. She was my greatest encouragement. She saw me with all my faults, liked me, and loved me. She believed in me when I didn't believe in myself. My sister's greatest gift to me was her time. She took the time to know me, understand me, encourage me, and love me. She told me that it was myself and her best friend Vanessa who taught her how to truly love a person for who they are and not what we want them to be. She was real, honest, fearless, ambitious, and humble. She was a fighter for those she loved. She was also a fighter for those overlooked and under-valued. She was a Jesus lover just like our parents taught us to be and she made no apologies for it. She was a musician, a singer, a rapper, a poet, a speaker, an author, a friend, an aunt, a sister, a daughter, a colleague, a role model, a lover of life and people. She was a force to be reckoned with. She saw greatness in me that I recognized was in me but never knew how to share that with the world at large. Baby sis always knew I would change the world in a massive way and spoke into and over my life for over 20 years. She encouraged me to take risks and trust myself. It was hard for me, because I've been physically, emotionally, socially and mentally beaten down for years and never believed in my shine nor my power. But Sherrie did. I didn't know what my life was going to look like, feel like, or sound like without her on this earth with me. But I was about to find out.

My sister's death brought me sadness but also brought me strength. In all honesty, I feel that it would have been possible to learn the lesson of living on purpose, believing in oneself, without my sister dying, but the will of God had to be accomplished. She saved me. God saved my life through the death of my sister. Some people might not like that statement, but I know personally what her life and her death did for me. A long time ago, she had shared a dream with me that she and I were in a burning building and the only way for us to survive was if I jumped. The building began to burn with more intensity, but I was too afraid to jump. The thieves of productivity, success, and growth kept me from jumping. Let me remind you what they are: fear, doubt, procrastination, and stagnancy. She told me that in the dream she said to me, "Kim, jump or I'm going to die," but I could not jump; I just could not. The dream ended but it was never determined if I jumped or not. I ask you my readers, did I jump?

The value of this pain and this valley experience showed me that everything in life is for a purpose: the bad, good, and indifferent. Sherrie's value, purpose, and impact are continuing posthumously. This valley experience enforced the importance of being in the present moment with life instead of yearning for tomorrow and what's next. The word of God tells us in Matthew 6:34 that we should not worry about tomorrow, for tomorrow will bring its own worries. Understanding the power of my TODAY has been transformational in how I treat people, how I live, who I spend time with, how I think, who I love, and how I love. The power of my today determines what I eat, who I choose to love and be in relationship with, the types of jobs or career paths I choose, the people I choose to have around me, the problems I choose to tackle, and the intent in which I live my life. I live my life with intent and on purpose because TODAY could be all that I have. Sherrie and I used to have this phrase we said to each other, DO IT NOW! There is no substitute for losing someone we love; however, we can channel what we feel into creating a more positive and impactful life. Circumstances in life can either make us BETTER or BITTER. We get to choose.

I am a stronger, more fearless, more courageous, more generous and forgiving human being because of my sister's death. Her death has fired up my will to live on purpose and authentically. It gives me permission to feel the fear and do it anyway. It has allowed me to learn the art of prioritizing. It has taught me how to dream. It has pulled out of me things that were dormant for years. My sister's death has given me Life. DO IT NOW! DO IT NOW! DO IT NOW! Love is real. When you love someone, all that matters is what you know and believe about them. On the other side of my valley was a rainbow. There is a life that God has imagined for me that will blow my mind and render me utterly speechless. But it can't and won't happen if I don't DO IT NOW!

Thank you to my family for accepting me as one of you, even though I drive you all crazy and am very different from all of you. Thank you for embracing the enigma that is Kim and Aunty Kim. Know this, fam, I will go through the fire for you! You are my gifts! I only hope that Sherrie will continue to bring out the best in us individually and collectively. Thank you to my friends and loved ones for your prayers and support. Thank you to Dr. Jackie's Writers Academy and the cohort of authors. Our stories are relevant and must be shared with the world.

GRACE

Sonya Weir

Lord, Saints berate me.
They sometimes hate me.
They castigate me, ostracize me.
They even criticize the
Way you made me.
Your blood has washed me.
Your mercy saved me.
Your grace forgave me.
Your love redeemed me.
I love my lot,
The one you gave me

My fat, my wrinkles,
And fading dimples.
Nappy hair, Lord,
Who cares?
I love my lot.
The one I got.
Oh, God you made me.
My head, my hands, my feet.
All that lies betwixt beneath.
My eyes, my ears, my lips, and hips.
Calloused hands, ashy skin.
Oh, Lord, you win.

Made in your likeness
And in your image.
Every crevice, every curve.
Blessings, I don't deserve.
So, Lord, I love my lot.

The one I've got.

I love you, Lord.
I am your creation,

Body, mind and soul.
I embrace my whole
With jubilation,
No humiliation.

No complaining.
I'll keep on praising.
I stand reminded.
No condemnation.
Ain't no shame.
The cross has saved me.
Pronouncement!

CHAPTER 16
My Blessing
Ann-Marie La Ronde-Richard

Life has multiple paths. Though you may not have full control over the path that your life takes, I believe you have control over how you react to what you encounter on this path and how you emerge from it. Life also has ups and downs. The peaks may be met with contentment and satisfaction, while the valleys impose a challenge or struggle. In my experiences, focusing on the positive aspects of that struggle, the small crests, no matter how minuscule, and having a positive mindset, can give you the strength to overcome the dips.

I completed *CONVENT HIGH SCHOOL* and Sixth-form, a 2-yr community college in Dominica, and then taught at Convent High for one year. My mom was a nurse and I grew up hanging out with her on the Children's ward at Princess Margaret Hospital and aspired to follow her footsteps in caring for others. I immigrated to the US in 1991 to further my education. Choosing to major in biology/premed at Suffolk University in Boston was not coincidental. The experiences gained at Princess Margaret Hospital developed my inner core and passion. I had a deep desire to make a difference in patients' lives, to heal their sickness, to make their lives better.

Life's path has a tendency to meander and change often with no warning or precursory tale. In my second year of college, I was diagnosed with a mild case of Lupus. This was not in the plan. My first impulse was to start researching this autoimmune disease and learn as much and as quickly as possible. I recall my anxiety and fear associated with the unknown. I learned Lupus is a chronic autoimmune disease in which a person's immune system mistakenly attacks healthy tissue, causing variable and quite unpredictable symptoms. For me, it was extensive joint pain and fatigue. As I continued to dive deeper into the vast amount of information publicly available on the disease, my heart skipped when I came across an article and read the word "terminal". I can recall feeling the tears run down my face as I thought my life was over. I remember feeling fear, anger, sadness, and asking, "Why me?" Just a year prior, I felt like I was the chosen one – being the first among my siblings to have the opportunity to go to a four-year college. My parents put their primary residence up as collateral against my student loan. Now, with the diagnosis of Lupus, I felt like God had left me behind. It took me a week before I had the courage to call my parents and share with them my news. I remember I kept my composure and I toned it down so as not to alarm them.

I felt like this valley in my life's path had the power to be all consuming. I did go through a short period of distress and doubt; however, my strong conviction for learning and deep passion for others quickly changed my trajectory. I realized how fortunate I was after further research and hearing of the experiences of other Lupus patients,

Thankfully, my symptoms were rather mild and bearable. I got strength from knowing that I was not alone and the realization that there were others, far less fortunate than I, who were suffering from the disease. I developed a feeling of gratefulness. Rather than allowing my diagnosis to slow me down, the pace of my life sped up. Thinking that the disease was fatal, I felt like I had to fulfill my purpose before being overcome. God had blessed me with an unimaginable amount of love and affection, coupled with infinite patience. I felt I needed to dissipate some of this.

Having a family before my condition worsened was a priority. Fortunately, God had placed an angel in my life, my life partner, and in 1996, one year after completing my undergraduate education, we were married. My first son, a blessing, came the following year in April. A blessing, indeed, as Lupus often flares up during pregnancy. I, however, had what seemed like 'a healing'. I experienced no flare ups or symptoms of the disease and miraculously, I had two more successful pregnancies. I am very fortunate, with 26 years behind me from my original diagnosis, and to date have not been on any pharmaceutical medications for my Lupus - since my first pregnancy.

The aforementioned circumstances led to another twist in my life's path. My desired career path of following in my mother's footsteps of becoming a medical professional changed. The reality of medical school seemed too demanding to take on while trying to raise a family. I, instead, attended graduate school to become a scientist. I completed my PhD in Pathology at Boston University, as well as a two-year post-doc program to become an Instructor of Medicine.

In 2007, I transferred from academia to the pharmaceutical industry. I started at Wyeth, which soon became Pfizer through an acquisition. Academia seemed too far removed from my purpose. The research seemed too basic. In industry, I would be able to focus on developing drugs to cure diseases and make people well again, thus being able to fulfill my childhood dream and returning to my passion. I enjoyed my job. I was doing early validation of drug targets that could potentially become a life-saving medicine for some. I worked every day with a purpose. Unfortunately, as I dove deeper into my research, I quickly realized the nature of drug development as a slow process and the low rate of conversion of an idea to a therapeutic was frustrating. I felt a sense of insufficiency and a lack of control. I knew that God had a bigger purpose for me.

In 2013, I co-founded the DOMINICAN HEALTH AND EDUCATION INITIATIVE (DAHEI), a 501(c)(3) non-profit organization with the mission to help enhance healthcare and educational capacity in Dominica to allow families to receive the quality services that they deserved. I also sought-after local volunteer opportunities to work in the community, primarily in roles that involved speaking and interacting directly with patients. I wanted to understand their needs and how I could help fulfill them. This led to a reminder – a reminder that this was indeed my life's path, and that I was walking in my purpose to do this full time. I found myself staying up at nights thinking of how I could fulfill my passion, fulfill 'God's mission for me', and be able to support myself and my family.

I started speaking to people within my network and the most important advice I got was to find a mentor, a sponsor, a career/life coach. Some of these terminologies are used interchangeably, but the point was to find someone who could provide guidance to help me sort out my current career dilemma. I was fortunate to have landed multiple mentors and career coaches, who, in combination with their different mentorship styles and networks, had a major impact on my career. One of my mentors was instrumental in helping me expand my network and inspired me to build long-term relationships. I learned by doing this, the other person can see value in having you in their network; not to just look for what you can gain from a relationship but also thinking of what you can offer to make it mutually beneficial and reciprocal. These are the most sustainable and most productive of relationships. Another mentor advised me to discuss my career aspirations with my current supervisor to fully accept that a career-change was what I was really yearning for. This was the best advice I received. Part of accepting this change was being able to communicate openly about it, including it in my career development plan, and discussing it with my supervisor. A good supervisor should take pride in helping employees meet their career goals. This led to a massive expansion of my networks, as the more individuals I spoke to, I was introduced to additional connections. A key take away for me was the realization that we are all people with similar challenges; many who shared similar interests as I or they, too, underwent a career change and could provide insight on what they experienced. In the end, it all worked out and in an intentional way.

In April of 2017, my department went through a major reorganization and several colleagues were impacted. I, too, was one of the scientists slated to be laid off. Coincidentally, during this time, there was also a shift in the pharmaceutical industry. The focus was to be more "Patient-Centric." We, scientists, previously thought to know what patients wanted, were now beginning to realize that patients knew best what they feel and experience with their diseases. Companies were beginning to create specific roles to enhance the patient experience: Patient Advocates. Across the industry, patient advocacy roles were in high demand. The news of my role elimination as a scientist closed one door but the shift in industry opened the door for me to return to my life's passion: patient care. This God-driven change in the medical sector created a pathway for my career to truly advocate for persons with unmet health needs. We were finally bringing the voice of the patient forward to our development programs.

Experiencing this life shift demonstrated the benefits of seeking out mentors, regardless of the level in your career or in your life. Mentors come from all walks of life. They do not need to understand your specific line of work, nor do they need to be at the pinnacle of their own careers to coach you. Sometimes, we have a secret "sponsor," without even asking, someone who supports us and lobbies on our behalf, and who serves as a silent reference. We just need to be open, aware, and curious to allow in those unsuspecting silent partners.

I have been extremely fortunate and blessed throughout my life. I experienced a short period of despair and anxiety with my Lupus diagnosis, which I could have allowed to consume me but I persevered. I took each dip that my life's path introduced and focused on the positives to guide me to the next peak. I believe that this recent success in my career as a patient advocate is truly my calling. This chapter in my life allows me to live the life of purpose that I have so yearned for: to be able to inspire others and bring them comfort. By sharing my story, I hope to influence others to seek out the positive aspects of whatever challenge they may encounter and convert that into strength that will support them and keep them from falling too deep into their valleys.

Always remember: life has multiple paths, but it is what we do on those paths that define us - Rise up and flourish!

"It doesn't matter how slowly you go as long as you do not stop."

-Confucius

ABOUT THE CO-AUTHORS

James Black

James Black is the author of WALDO *and the* RAMBLINGS ON MAN. The author and poet is a trained teacher, former talk show host, semi-professional soccer player, avid reader, inspirational speaker and an amateur guitarist. James' love for classical literature and poetry has resulted in his unique writing style, bolstered by his intriguing insight. His work is as warm and colorful as his tropical origins.

James uses cleverness and adroit to bring life to his non-fiction pieces. With a knack for retelling stories, James is sure to inform and thrill in the process. Find out more about his future works @AUTHORJAMESBLACK on Instagram.

Seanna M. Bowen

Seanna is a loving mother to Sarah and Abigail, who serve as her constant motivation to succeed in life. She earned her B.A. in Public Policy and Government at EASTERN CONNECTICUT STATE UNIVERSITY and is currently pursuing a Master's Degree in Human Services with a concentration in Clinical Counseling. Seanna has over 10 years' experience in the Human Services field, and recently branched out by starting her own company which will provide home based health care services to individuals in need.

She is an active volunteer in the West Indian community of Greater Hartford, and through her work, has helped increase the awareness and focus of West Indian cultural, social, political and educational activities. Seanna is also an on-air media personality and has hosted and been featured on various local radio and television shows. In addition, she is a writer and content editor for the premier Caribbean website, **JAMAICANS.COM.**

Alanna Chambers

Alanna is a Product Manager at an insurance company in Hartford, CT. Healthcare. She is an eBusiness strategist partnering with business partners to conceptualize new digital experiences, develop business cases in support of needed funding, and oversee the build out of the digital experience. She has 20 years' experience in the financial, insurance and healthcare industry. She earned an MBA in Entrepreneurial Thinking & Innovative Practices, as well as, an MS in Communications and Information Management. She is currently pursuing a PhD in Organizational Leadership with a focus on Information Technology. She is passionate about diversity and inclusion and believes that we can think independently together.

Dr. Jackie Evans Phillips

D. Jackie Evans-Phillips, **Your Mid-Wife of Purpose**, is on a mission to create an empowerment movement to awaken individuals to their **Call to Greatness**. Making a difference in the lives of others has become Dr. Jackie's life mission.

Dr. Jackie is the founder and owner of **Life Changers Consulting LLC**, a company that provides life empowerment, writing and publishing services to individuals who are ready to say "Yes" to Greatness. Dr. Jackie's signature program is **The Soaring Into Greatness Writing Institute**. During this 9-month journey, she empowers her clients to make meaning of their life's journey by writing a chapter for her book project or they may opt to write their individual book. This process enables her clients to develop a sense of legacy and establish their brand which will impact their families, communities, and generations to come.

Dr. Jackie invites you to be part of this journey where she will take you on the journey of writing; developing and publishing your book; as well as establishing your brand. During this process, you will be coached through the writing, publishing, branding and marketing processes. For more information, please contact us at info@drjackiephillips.com or visit **our website** **WWW.DRJACKIEPHILLIPS.COM**

Kimberly Gordon

Kimberly Gordon is a counselor, educator, writer, public speaker, philanthropist, and social entrepreneur. She is a certified school counselor in New York State and Georgia and has over seven years of experience in higher Education, Teaching and Counseling. She served as a teacher for five years in charter, public, and private schools, and currently works as an Elementary School Counselor in New York City.

Gordon delivers life skill enhancement and community resource linkage to students and their families. She provides individual and group counseling to students. She has certification in *Conflict Resolution, Mental Illness and Addictive Disorders, Suicide Risk Assessment, Cultural Competence and Recovery Principles, Mental Health First Aid, Dignity for Students Act and Therapeutic Crisis Intervention System.* She served as an advocate for individuals with intellectual and development disabilities and is passionate about the work of facilitating the growth and development of individuals academically, socially, emotionally, physically, professionally, spiritually, and financially.

Kimberly received her *M.S. in Counseling and Guidance and an Advanced Certificate in Family Counseling and Mental Health Counseling* from Long Island University in Brooklyn, New York. She received her *B.A. in Psychology* from DICKINSON COLLEGE in Carlisle, Pennsylvania. Ms. Gordon maintains several organizational memberships including ASSOCIATION OF SCHOOL COUNSELOR ASSOCIATION, AMERICAN COUNSELING ASSOCIATION and NEW YORK SCHOOL COUNSELOR ASSOCIATION.

Kimberly was born to Beverly and Dorrick Gordon and is one of four siblings: two sisters and one brother, Jacqueline, Sherrie, and Derrick. Kimberly lost her younger sister Sherrie in 2015 and has honored her by writing this chapter. Kimberly is aunt to Daniel, Joseph and Matthew Elleston. Kimberly enjoys listening to audio books and music, spending time with family and friends, dancing, encouraging others, and being a Born-Again Christian. Kimberly also finds fulfillment and purpose working on her blog **MSGORDONENCOURAGES** on *WORDPRESS*, sharing encouragement on her Instagram page @MSGORDONENCOURAGES, and the creation of her encouragement and empowerment company TURN TO YOU CREATIONS, LLC.

Crystal Hamer

Crystal Hamer, Chief Design Officer of *THE CAMERON TYLER NETWORK*, is originally from Springfield, Massachusetts. She currently resides in Bloomfield, Connecticut. Her business, which specializes in proofreading and customized curriculum design services, is named after her son who she miscarried in August, 2012. She is an educator with over 20 years of experience as a middle school *ELA* teacher and *JOB CORPS* contractor administrator.

Sascia Hayden

With each new experience in her life, Sascia Hayden tries to share her experiences with others whether family, friends or new persons she meets, as encouragement and a life lesson.

Born in Jamaica, she spent the first 16 years of her life there and was educated through high school there. She then joined her parents and extended family who had previously immigrated to the United States. This was a culture shock. The transition was difficult as Sascia entered community college at 16, and by age 20, she graduated with a B.A. in *MANAGEMENT INFORMATION SYSTEMS*. By 22, she completed her MBA in *INTERNATIONAL BUSINESS* and is completing a second Master's degree in *EDUCATION TECHNOLOGY*.

As an instructional designer/developer for over eight years, Sascia aims to design learning experiences that present information in an engaging manner, easily understood and applicable. Using technology, her creative power is fully evident in her interactive learning modules which range from online courses, videos, virtual classes to interactive reference modules, all while promoting self-learning at the individual's own pace.

Sacsia values opportunities to volunteer. As SECRETARY OF THE PUTNAM CONDOMINIUMS, she ensures the condo owners receive periodic association communication updates. She volunteers at her local church as marketing designer and event coordinator. She worked with a missionary group, MOUNTAINS OF HOPE FOR HAITI, as an assistant web designer.

Along with her passion for learning, Sascia enjoys her many hobbies which include running, tennis, and traveling.

Sascia can be reached at SASCIAHAYDEN@GMAIL.COM or on LinkedIn at **HTTP://LINKEDIN.COM/IN/SASCIA-HAYDEN-315B4114A.**

Ann-Marie La Ronde-Richard

Ann-Marie La Ronde-Richard is a Patient Engagement Lead in the Internal Medicine Research Unit at PFIZER, a role that allows her to work more closely with patients. Having previously worked as a scientist for 10 years at PFIZER, Ann-Marie is now in a unique position to help bridge the gap between scientists and patients, ensuring that scientists better understand the unmet needs of diverse patient groups, what symptoms they experience with their disease and what they desire in new therapies. With this career transition, Ann-Marie has gotten immense gratification and is now 'living a life of purpose.' By sharing her story, she hopes to inspire others to take the bold steps necessary to get to a place where they, too, can fulfill their purpose.

Ann-Marie was born and raised on the beautiful island of Dominica in the Eastern Caribbean and migrated to the United States in 1991 to further her education. She obtained her B.S.

degree from *SUFFOLK UNIVERSITY* in Boston and then completed her Doctorate in Pathology at *BOSTON UNIVERSITY SCHOOL OF MEDICINE*. Ann-Marie credits her amazing husband and three beautiful children for her ability to gain strength, rather than refuge, from an early diagnosis with a life-threatening illness.

In 2007, after post-doctoral training and a 1-yr assignment as Instructor of Medicine, Ann-Marie moved from *BOSTON UNIVERSITY* to *PFIZER*, a decision driven by her strong desire to work in a role where she could, more directly, impact the lives of patients.

Having now fulfilled her educational and career dreams, AnnMarie wants to help others live healthier and more fulfilling lives. She is the cofounder of the *DOMINICAN HEALTH AND EDUCATION INITIATIVE* (DAHEI), a 501c3 organization focused on improving the quality of life for families in her Native island, Dominica through enhancing education and healthcare.

Jarmaine V. Lee

Passionate and enthusiastic about life, **Jarmaine V. Lee** has spent his life building self-esteem in youth and young adults across the country. As an advocate for change within communities stretching from Urban and Suburban Chicago all the way through Seattle to Hartford, Mr. Lee is tirelessly building his community one person at a time. His most prized and valuable treasures are his wife, children, and his grandchild! Ultimately, his goal is to reach all the lives along his path that are need of positivity and motivation to overcome!

Reverend Matha Telca Ouellette

Reverend Ouellette is a retired teacher from St. Lucia. She taught at *CARMEN RENÉ MEMORIAL ELEMENTARY SCHOOL*, for 22 years. As she taught, she mothered her students as though they were her own. After retiring, she immigrated to the United States in 2004.

Reverend Ouellette is a well-grounded Christian. At a young age, she desired to be set apart from the norm and at 13 she fully surrendered her life to the Lord. Reverend Ouellette felt she had a different mindset than her peers. She believed she was born to serve the Lord, Jesus Christ. During her early years as a follower of Jesus Christ, she sensed the Lord was calling her into service. After many years of refusing her call to ministry, she accepted and became a certified ordained minister in the CHURCH OF GOD of Cleveland, Tennessee. Reverend Ouellette is authorized to preach, teach, and defend the gospel of Jesus Christ and other such ministerial duties as authorized by the INTERNATIONAL GENERAL ASSEMBLY OF THE CHURCH OF GOD. She is now an associate pastor under the leadership of Bishop Wesley Beason.

Presently, she conducts and teaches Bible study and Sunday school programs at her church, MT. CARMEL CHURCH OF GOD. Her desire is to develop and educate the people of God and to encourage them to approve themselves by studying the Word of God. Apart from her enthusiasm to know and teach the Word of God, she is also an intercessor. She spends many hours in prayer, battling on her knees in combat with principalities, spiritual wickedness, and powers of darkness. Her goal is to reach the masses at any cost for the Kingdom of God.

Monique Taylor

Monique Taylor, M.S. is a trailblazer, wife, author, educator, motivational speaker, educational consultant, and life-long learner. She is a proud native of Hartford, Connecticut with extensive knowledge in the nonprofit sector and in education throughout the Greater Hartford Area and expert in youth development strategies, and program development.

Monique holds a graduate degree from CENTRAL CONNECTICUT STATE UNIVERSITY with a Master's in Counseling with a specialization *in Student Development in Higher Education*, and a Bachelor's degree from EASTERN CONNECTICUT STATE UNIVERSITY in *Communications*.

Ainsworth Thompson

Mr. Thompson believes that all things are possible for those who have faith and anyone can accomplish whatever they dream. He is an active member in the community and exhibits extensive leadership skills in training, coaching, and motivating people to achieve their goals. He used his gift of motivation while owning and running his own real estate finance business where he employed members of the community and helped thousands obtain home ownership.

Ainsworth attended CENTRAL CONNECTICUT STATE UNIVERSITY where he earned a B.A., majoring in Economics with a minor in Finance, Accounting, and Marketing. He has studied Theology at THE HARTFORD SEMINARY and attained a Master's of Science in Real Estate (MSRE) from ROOSEVELT UNIVERSITY, served on Community Advisory Board for CONNECTICUT PUBLIC TELEVISION (CPTV) and NATIONAL PUBLIC RADIO (NPR) and has served as an inspirational columnist in the West Indian American newspaper serving the central Connecticut area.

 He is a member of the WEST INDIAN SOCIAL CLUB and has taken a leadership role in many activities including HARTFORD'S WEST

INDIAN PARADE and the TASTE OF THE CARIBBEAN FESTIVAL. He is a columnist for the *WEST INDIAN AMERICAN* newspaper and contributing writer for the *NEW EAST SIDE* newspaper.

K. Stephen Wilson

Mr. Wilson graduated from SOUTHERN CONNECTICUT STATE UNIVERSITY in 2002 with a B.S. in *Social Work* and a minor in *Psychology*. Stephen developed a passion for working with at-risk youth and their families, as well as for the development of leadership within young men. A favorite quote states that *"IT IS EASIER TO BUILD STRONG CHILDREN THAN TO REPAIR BROKEN MEN,"*

-FREDERICK DOUGLASS.

Because of this and his faith and commitment to God, he has been moved to mentor youth and advocate for student success. He has worked as a Juvenile Detention Officer, with foster care agencies, as Counseling Manager at the HARTFORD JOB CORPS ACADEMY, and currently at ACHIEVEMENT FIRST HARTFORD MIDDLE SCHOOL as a Behavior Specialist. Working with the at-risk population has required additional skills to be served which has led him to seek additional education/certifications. Mr. Wilson became a Certified Youth Life Coach/Mentor in 2016 and is currently enrolled at the UNIVERSITY OF SAINT JOSEPH pursuing his Masters of Social Work.

He serves as the Music & Arts Director of the REHOBOTH CHURCH OF GOD in Bloomfield, Connecticut, where he assists creating uplifting and impactful worship services. He serves in the Boys Club ministry.

Madonna Lilburn-Thompson has been a licensed cosmetologist for 25 years. Today she owns a hair salon business, BEAUTY SECRETS HAIR SALON in East Hartford, Connecticut where she currently resides. Accompanying her are her four daughters and husband. Growing up, she immigrated to the United States from the beautiful island of Saint Lucia. Moving to the state of Connecticut at the tender age of nine, she continued her education. Throughout her coming of age years, she attended Weaver High School. Madonna then discovered her passion for being a cosmetician and fulfilled her career goal of being a licensed cosmetician, later also becoming a contracted hair stylist at a number of healthcare facilities within Connecticut. *The Power of the Valley* is her first publication.

Sonya Weir

""Your imagination is the canvas for life's color-filled landscapes" and "Your imagination is the reel for life's unwinding adventures"

Sonya Weir is a poet by nature and a writer by passion. Her craft reflects her free-spiritedness. She is as free as the words she pens, untamed as her doodling and limitless as the air she breathes. From an early age, writing has been her vessel of escape and exploration. It is the tool she uses to forge beauty out of ashes; to reflect purpose in the seemingly insignificant; to create moments that take our breath away.

Sonya, a native of Jamaica, is the sixth of seven children. She was educated at Shortwood Teachers College, Jamaica, Capital Community College, Eastern Connecticut State University, Central Connecticut State University and Cambridge College. Her immediate family comprises her son Sean, his friend Candy (Sanike) and grand dog Bella.

Sonya loves hard, gives generously, and expects nothing. She lives her best life when helping others through words, a hug, a helping hand and a listening ear. Her fundamental thought: 'When you have done much, there is not much to say. Say it quickly and succinctly."

Sonya enjoys hearing from her readers. You may contact her via email at weirsonya@gmail.com.

T'challa Williams

Born in Hartford, **T'challa Williams** has always loved the arts. She has performed on stages since elementary school, and continues throughout her adulthood. Her passion has led her to include writing with her performing. With two books of poetry completed and a third on the way, she has given her voice to nonfiction and boldly shared a piece of her story. This widowed, mother of six is looking forward to continuing to tell her truth. As an author and poet, this fearless artist is going non-stop. T'challa believes that everyone has a gift that is to be used to make people better. "We are here to lift one another up to the level God intended. There is great joy to be had in advancing another; we must embrace it transparently to truly see our growth."

15302091R00097

Made in the USA
Middletown, DE
20 November 2018